FROM HERZ TO HILTON

TO BE OR NOT TO BE A JEW

ERNEST A. HILTON

MENSCH PUBLISHING

CONTENTS

Publisher: Mensch Publishing

In loving memory of Eugene (Jenö) Por, my stepfather, who survived both World Wars and the horrors of both Westerbork and Buchenwald camps, living an extraordinary life of 105 years. Loved and respected by all and who inspired me to travel and experience the wonders of the modern world.

AUTHOR'S NOTE

I was born Ernst Adolf Herz in 1932, with the world already in the midst of the Depression and beginning the age of Hitler and the Nazi Party. In 1933, Hitler decreed that all German Jews were to be denationalized. That meant we had no identity in Germany or anywhere else. My parents took the threat of statelessness seriously and decided to move as refugees to the Netherlands. The Dutch, in 1933, were accommodating, and that is how we got to live in Aerdenhout near Zandvoort at the North Sea.

By 1932, the Nazis were the largest political party in the Reichstag. In January of the following year, with no other leader able to command sufficient support to govern, President Paul von Hindenburg appointed Hitler chancellor of Germany. Shortly thereafter, a fire broke out in the Reichstag building in Berlin, and authorities arrested a young Dutch communist who confessed to starting it. Hitler used this episode to convince

Hindenburg to declare an emergency, suspending many civil liberties throughout Germany, including freedom of the press, freedom of expression, and the right to hold public assemblies. The police were authorized to detain citizens without cause, and the authority usually exercised by regional governments became subject to control by Hitler's national regime.

Almost immediately, Hitler began dismantling German democratic institutions and imprisoning or murdering his chief opponents. When Hindenburg died the following year, Hitler took the titles of Fuhrer, chancellor, and commander-in-chief of the army. He expanded the army tremendously, reintroduced conscription, and began developing a new air force—all violations of the Treaty of Versailles.

Hitler's military spending and ambitious public-works programs, including building a German autobahn, helped restore prosperity. His regime also suppressed the Communist Party and purged his own paramilitary storm troopers, whose violent street demonstrations alienated the German middle class. The bloodletting—called the "Night of the Long Knives"—was hugely popular and welcomed by the middle class as a blow struck for law and order. In fact, many Germans went along with the full range of Hitler's policies, convinced that they would ultimately be advantageous for the country.

In 1938, Hitler began his long-promised expansion of national boundaries to incorporate ethnic Germans. He colluded with Austrian Nazis to orchestrate the Anschluss, the annexation of Austria to Germany.

And in Hitler's most brazenly aggressive act yet, Czechoslovakia was forced to surrender the Sudetenland, a mountainous border region populated predominantly by ethnic Germans. The Czechs looked to Great Britain and France for help, but hoping to avoid war—they had been bled white in World War I—these nations chose a policy of appeasement. At a conclave held at Munich in September 1938, representatives of Great Britain and France compelled Czech leaders to cede the Sudetenland in return for Hitler's pledge not to seek additional territory. The following year, the German army swallowed up the remainder of Czechoslovakia.

British Prime Minister Neville Chamberlain, one of the signers of the Munich pact, had taken Hitler at his word. Returning to Britain with this agreement in hand, he proudly announced that he had achieved "peace with honor. I believe it is peace for our time."

A year later, in 1939, German troops stormed into Poland.

And here, as Germany is about to begin its blitzkrieg against Poland, is where I want to stop this familiar narrative of World War II and talk about religion. I am a survivor of Westerbork transit camp, a temporary collection point for Jews in the Netherlands, before we were sent to concentration camps. I am also a survivor of Bergen-Belsen. I was sent to these places because I am a

Jew. I was only a child and had committed no crimes except to be born a Jew. But I separate my Jewishness from my religion. Let me explain.

Leo Tolstoy's last book, *The Kingdom of God Is Within You,* is a key text for proponents of nonviolence. Tolstoy meant to abolish violence, even the defensive kind, and to give up revenge.

"How can you kill people, when it is written in God's commandment: 'Thou shalt not murder?'"

I like Tolstoy's philosophic idea of "The kingdom of God is within you," rather than in places of worship. If we want to have a peaceful world, then Tolstoy's ideas are the only way I can see that can bring peace on earth.

The question is whether the pacifism of a Tolstoy could withstand a Hitler. One thing is certain: if there is a God, it needed to be found within everybody to get through the violence of World War II.

To tell you the truth, I turned atheist after the war because I figured that God didn't do anything for the six million Jews who were removed from the earth. But "the kingdom of God is within you" has stuck with me, and it is the only religion that makes sense.

But my atheism is separate from my Jewishness. In the camps, I kept asking myself why my family and I were caught up in this misery. I always got the same answer, and that was, "You are a Jew."

Later, I changed my name from Herz to Hilton—and I will explain why in these pages—but it was never to escape my Jewishness. Irrespective of my new name, I was a Jew from a family with a very long Jewish history.

And it is in that history that I draw inner strength—the "Kingdom of God" that is inside me.

As I write this at age eighty-eight, I am in good physical and mental condition as well as a survivor of the Holocaust. I, therefore, persuaded myself that I had a sufficiently interesting life story to write about it. So, here I am writing. Like everyone, I had my ups and downs. My extraordinary life experience was to survive for three-and-a-half years of concentration camps during WWII in both Holland and Germany from age nine to thirteen.

The gnawing issue I struggle with is why Jews were being picked on and thus ended in camps or far worse destinations for those multitudes who were killed in gas chambers Nazis built to eradicate Jewishness in Europe. After much tinkering with my Jewish question, my issue can be expressed in a nutshell as: "To be or not to be a Jew?"

Today, I still am not ready to answer that question.

1

EARLY CHILDHOOD

As I grew up—in a household with a mother, father, and a sister who was four years older—I gradually understood what they listened to on the radio from Germany was bad news.

My father was certain that if Germany started a World War II, they wouldn't overrun Holland because it was considered neutral in WWI. My father assumed that neutrality would occur again.

The Dutch Government gave us permission to start a new residence in Holland, and we chose Aerdenhout. This was an easy train commute to Amsterdam, where my father started a new business with our neighbor Jupp Weiss, who was also a German Jew. Weiss had a wife and two sons. We settled down easily in our three-story house at 42 Dahlialaan, Aerdenhout. We had a small garden in the front of our house and a small garden in the rear that ended at a creek. Across from the creek was a pasture with grazing cows.

Since I was barely one year old when I arrived in Aerdenhout, I must skip to four or five years old before I can dig into my earliest memories. At that stage, I was well aware of our German Nanny Erna Rosenthal, who was Jewish and originated from Cuxhaven near Hamburg. My sister, Erica, was enchanted with Erna, and this loving relationship lasted many years after the war.

At age three or four, I started playing with my large collection of miniature cars, which I pushed with great precision over our carpets from one end to the other of our living room. I was also allowed to play outside with Klaus Weiss, our neighbor who was three or four years older, but we got along well. By then, I was given the loving nickname of Burschi. I was given a miniature wheelbarrow and shovel, and I turned myself into what in Dutch would be called Straat Beleideging (street management). I had seen a job waiting for me. With my shovel, I picked up all the horse droppings from our street into my wheelbarrow and then distributed those droppings up and down my street so that each garden got a portion! Did our neighbors accept my "generosity" on behalf of the environment? I never found out. Nor did anyone not accept my daily gifts! Perhaps because they recognized my activity on behalf of a cleaner environment? Since there were daily regular horse-drawn vendors such as the Milk Boer, vegetable, or the fish vendor, I did my daily duty conscientiously because I liked the easy routine.

My street management made me friends with the various horse-drawn cart vendors, and often they would let me ride on the horses' drivers' bench all the way to the end of the street. That was a privilege for a little boy.

On the occasion of Yom Kippur, the holiest of all Jewish religious holidays, my sister told me I must fast. As fate would have it, the fish vendor arrived and invited me for a ride on his cart and handed me a medium-sized, green pickle. It was crispy and sour, and I liked it a lot, so I ate the whole pickle on an empty stomach. Yes, that was sort of a really bad sin. I am glad to say that it didn't bother me; instead, I was grateful for the pickle, and my mother didn't mind me breaking the fast.

Speaking of food, Erna was, in addition to a loved nanny, also a great cook and my favorite main course dish was a beef stew into which I dunked pieces of bread until it was soaking wet and then stuffed it in my mouth with a great squashy bite that dribbled a bit down my chin. For dessert, any dessert was welcome, but more so if it was served with warm custard sauce. Erna cooked everything: breakfast, lunch, and dinner. I think my mother had no sense of cooking but probably discussed the daily main dinner menu with Erna, and she would do the shopping.

Transportation in Holland was, and still is, via bicycle, and I used to sit on the little seat over the rear wheel of my mother's bike, just like a Peanuts character.

Naturally, I felt all the bumps. Subsequently, at age six or seven, I had learned to ride a bike, and on weekends the four of us would pedal around our neighborhood for fun.

Weekends in the summer also brought us by tram to Zandvoort at the North Sea. I enjoyed that beach destination because it always provided for a nice vanilla ice cream wedged between two thin crispy waffles. Like all children, I enjoyed being read stories. *Bruintje Beer* was my favorite. But I also liked cowboy stories, and these related to America, including American Indians. The best book of all turned out to be about Max and Moritz because it came in a cartoon type of book about two very naughty little boys.

By 1937, I started to go to school. I had picked up Dutch on the street and heard German at home, so I was sort of bilingual at an early age. I learned to sing Sinterklaas songs and the Piet Hein song. Sinterklaas is Dutch for Santa Claus, but the Dutch Christmas happens about a week earlier than Christmas in England and America. Sinterklaas always arrived with his white horse on a boat from Spain together with his helper *Zwarte Piet* (Black Peter), and they brought a lot of candy.

My worst event early at school was that I hit a girl on the playground, and it was reported to my mother. I was told to never do that again; my mother bought a nice box of chocolates, enabling me to make a peace offering to the girl who was happy with my gift. Because of that one incident, I suffered a lifetime habit of buying boxes of chocolates for girls.

In 1939, there was a worldwide Boy Scout Jamboree in Vogelesang near Aerdenhout. Erna took me to see thousands of Boy Scouts from around the world living in tents. But the highlight of this event was that I saw Dutch Queen Wilhelmina accompanied by her daughter Juliana arrive in her golden coach to give the opening speech at the Jamboree. The Golden Coach has a long history, and nowadays, it has even become controversial as the raw material for the carriage came from the Dutch East Indies when colonialism and slavery existed.

When I reached the age of seven, I picked up on war vibes from my mother and father, who heard on the radio that Hitler had taken over the German-speaking Sudetenland—a part of Czechoslovakia. That, alone, was deeply worrying to my mother, but my father was still fixated on neutrality. Not much later, the Nazis conquered the whole of Czechoslovakia. Hitler's next move was to annex Austria within Germany, and the Austrian government was more than happy about the Anschluss. Since annexation isn't warfare, everybody eased off in our household and throughout Europe.

However, on September 1, 1939, Germany aggressively attacked Poland, and after fierce fighting and the Molotov–Ribbentrop Pact, the Germans had managed to split Poland between themselves and the Soviets. The Second World War, without any doubt, had commenced, and it was to engulf all of Europe.

I don't know what my father thought after that, but there was a lot of friction in our household.

On May 10, 1940, our fears were confirmed because Germany invaded Holland on that day. My sister's voice still echoes in my ears all these years later. She came into my bedroom and, instead of her usual "good morning," she said, "The war has started!" All I knew was that I felt bad. I had no idea what warfare was.

My mother, with some degree of anger, told my father that his notion of World War I neutrality hadn't come true.

"The Nazis frightened us out of Germany, and now we are frightened of what Hitler intends to do with us the Jews in Holland," she said.

My grandparents were by now also refugees in Holland and residing in Amsterdam. They must have felt miserable to be caught in Holland while Germany had invaded. It took only four days for the German blitzkrieg to defeat the Dutch. Once the Nazis had grasped power in Holland, we learned quickly that they were also out to hunt Jews.

In 1941, we were told to get away from the coast. So, we moved to Hilversum. Being Jewish, we were forced to wear the Star of David sewn on our outerwear. Neither my sister Erica nor I were permitted to continue to go to school. So, we were cut off from our friends in Aerdenhout, we had no friends in Hilversum, and we were not going to school. That meant we loitered around until early 1942, when we were instructed to take the train to Westerbork.

When we arrived in Westerbork, our fears were even at a higher pitch because now we were in a concentration camp. Every week, a transport of Dutch Jews arrived in Westerbork, and after a while, transports of Dutch Jews were sent in cattle cars to what seemed to be a question of life and death.

Retroactively, arriving and settling in Aerdenhout was unknowingly the start of the Holocaust.

Ernest in Aerdenhout, the Netherlands, circa 1936

Erica and Ernest in Aerdenhout, The
Netherlands, circa 1936

Ernest in Zandvoort, the Netherlands, circa
1939.

Ernest in Zandvoort, the Netherlands, circa 1939.

Ernest, portrait photo, circa 1941

2

WESTERBORK

On January 15, 1942, we were sent from Hilversum to Westerbork, a transit camp where prisoners were gathered before being sent to concentration camps elsewhere. We were at Westerbork for about twenty-five months.

Prior to the selection of inmates for the first July 15, 1942, transport from Westerbork to "nowhere" (It turned out to have been to Auschwitz), the four of us, with other German Jews, were queued up in front of the camp commandant to be judged "to go/not to go."

We felt that the moment of death or survival was about to occur.

The Nazi camp commandant stood with his Jewish adviser, Jupp Weiss, our neighbor from Ardenhout, ready to select the condemned. When it was our turn to be judged, the four of us—my father, Walter Herz; my mother; Margot Herz Gumperz; my sister, Erica, age thirteen; and me, age nine, stood before the commandant.

Weiss spoke. He pointed to my father and said, "Walter Herz is a very capable and engaged worker in the camp administration; we can't lose him."

Then it was my mother's turn.

"Margot Herz is a very efficient and a popular barrack manageress, so we need her here," Weiss said.

The commandant looked us four over. Then he pronounced his verdict.

"The Herz family stays."

I hope my father thanked Weiss deliriously because we all assumed that going on the transport—with the advice to bring minimum belongings and then loaded into cattle wagons that were locked with a bang when the departure took place—implied a trip to nowhere good was on its way. And our fears were more than right because, after the war, we found out that all those transports did end up at a gas chamber facility in Poland. Around 95,000 Dutch Jews, many of whom were the descendants of those who had fled to Holland from either the Spanish or Portuguese Inquisitions, were now rolling weekly on a one-way trip to be killed.

Since we were one of the first people to occupy Westerbork from within Holland, we were settled in fairly nice wooden houses. Because Westerbork was secured by Dutch police and/or Dutch army personnel, my father succeeded in getting permission to return to Amsterdam for a day to buy some pots and pans that we needed. That was the last time he saw Amsterdam until we returned after the war.

One day a family of three—a husband, wife, and a three-year-old child—were mustered in our little wooden house because there was no room elsewhere. I don't know if they were Dutch or German, but what stuck in my mind was that the child managed to call me something like Enely (instead of Ernst), and I felt that this child became very devoted to me for no reason I can state but might have been for fear of what was about to happen.

They did not stay long in our wooden house but were sent on one of the early transports to the end of their lives.

Ever since then, I haven't been able to forget that child.

Very likely, all three of them were gassed to death in Auschwitz. In my mind, I see the procedure of being led into the gas chamber under the pretense of having a shower. Instead, they must have crumbled to the floor while dying from the gas. Jews were forced to do the dirty work, emptying the gas chamber and bringing the corpses into the crematoriums to be incinerated. That picture remained in my mind for the rest of my life. I have often shed tears when I remember that child.

There was no violence in Westerbork—even when it was the day of transportation. People who had been assigned for transport were surely extremely fearful of what lies ahead in their unknown destinations. As the officials slammed closed the doors of the cattle cars and then locked them, those of us left behind were also left with miserable visions of a destination from which there would be no escape.

In Westerbork, teenagers such as my sister got together and celebrated Jewish holidays. They knew some of the ritual prayers and Jewish dances, so they gathered to form some sense of community.

I didn't have any friends my age in Westerbork, but I do have vague memories of a lady who tried to be a teacher to all the children. As the camp grew in population, my mother was the manager in a barrack, and my father worked in an office within Westerbork. I stayed in that little wooden family house most of the time because there was nothing to do outside nor inside. I was too young to be given tasks, whereas my sister, who was fourteen, did get a job within the camps' so-called hospital, which was more like a clinic. She pricked fingers for blood tests.

Margot Gumperz's Westerbork registration card.

3

BERGEN-BELSEN

The Herz family escaped from the weekly transports until Westerbork was empty of the Dutch Jews. Thereafter, we, the German Jews, were told to get ready to be sent on February 15, 1944, in normal passenger trains to the Bergen-Belsen concentration camp.

Belsen was organized in an array of different camps. We ended up in Stern camp, and when we walked through the gate to the head-counting square, we noticed that Jupp Weiss was already there and, again, he was the Jewish adviser—this time to the Bergen-Belsen camp commandant. Before we were counted, Weiss told us that Belsen was a lot worse than Westerbork. He eased our minds by saying nobody was killed at Belsen, but we soon discovered that many died of disease, starvation, and overwork.

Weiss became famous after the war for his work on behalf of his fellow Jews at Westerbork and Bergen-

Belsen's Stern (Star) camp, particularly for children. He became a Jewish Elder, which became synonymous after the war with Nazi collaboration. Weiss was the exception and is universally recognized as somebody who truly cared about the Jews in his care. In a letter home to his family in 1945, he described celebrating Jewish holidays at the camp. During a Passover seder, he gave a speech:

"We are among the very few European Jews who might possibly survive extermination. We must stick it out because we have an obligation to take part in the rebuilding of the Jewish people. We have seen many nations perish, and the Jewish people have outlived them all. Even after this war, with all our personal sacrifices, the sun will shine for us again."

He described Passover songs sung by young children, writing, "Never had I heard them sung more beautifully than by these young voices."

In the thirteen months that we spent in the Stern camp of Bergen-Belsen, it gradually overloaded with ever more inmates—so many that two people were assigned to one bed on the three-layered bunkbeds. Erica and I slept foot to head in one bed. So, the hygiene went from bad to worse with fast-growing lice.

The first time I saw skin-covered skeletons on the ground was when I looked across at a women's barrack, and at least a dozen dead ones were piled up naked. Each morning, a cart would arrive and throw the skeletons on the wagon, and a horse would bring those cadavers presumably to a mass grave.

On each corner of Stern lager was a watchtower with one soldier on duty. Gossiping with the neighbors across the barbed wire was forbidden. Had we spoken to either of our neighbors, we would have been shot.

The barbed wire at the entrance of Stern was about twice the height of an average male. One day, a man who was perhaps mentally ill started to climb up the barbed wire fence to get out. He was shot on the way up. I was not upset about it because I didn't know who he was. I didn't hang around waiting for the body to be removed.

One day, my grandfather Benno Gumperz, age eighty-five, returned from the latrine, and he collapsed from a heart attack and died on the spot. He had suffered from angina for decades. A horse and a cart arrived, and we accompanied him out of Stern gate. That was the last that we saw of him. At least he had a painless death. I don't remember if my mother was upset at the death of her father, but perhaps she expected it to happen in Belsen.

An average-size American lives off 2,500 calories and 1,500 calories if he wants to lose weight. I am guessing that in Belsen, our calories per day amounted to more or less 700 calories, which would cause a grownup to die from starvation. And that is exactly what happened in Belsen. There was little in the way of violent death, but people died from hard work, little food, and death from starvation. I had seen the corpses from across Stern camp, but I am unaware of people dying in our barrack and being transported to a mass grave.

My biggest fear was the daily 7 a.m. headcount (*Appel* in German), where everyone had to exit from their barracks, line up, and wait for hours until the officers finished the count. This happened in whatever weather we had, and a lot of the time, it was winter. Nobody got hit or abused, but still, there were a lot of commands being shouted in German to make the *Appel* work. My grandmother, suffering from cancer, was allowed to stay in her bunk. I suppose other sick people were counted while in bed.

I didn't starve to death, but I couldn't grow because I was extremely undernourished. Realizing that my mother couldn't fix my hunger, I pretended that I wasn't hungry. That pretense is the way to move toward starvation. So, food was a constant topic even if we couldn't get better rations.

Late in our time at Bergen-Belsen, some of our German staff were sent to the front to fight. Taking their place were German criminals known as kapos. In general, they managed things with lots of violence. One day, a kapo got sick and, knowing we had a nurse in our barrack, asked for help. The nurse agreed to heal him and brought out her syringe. She had filled it with air instead of medication, and he died on the spot.

Once, I found a kapo's truncheon on the ground outside and brought it to my mother. I reasoned that if I were to hide it, the kapo could no longer beat anybody with it. I was slowly starving, so I likely did not even realize the danger I was putting myself in. I didn't fear death, but I feared violence.

Meanwhile, ever more inmates came into Stern lager, and we were forced two to a bunk. That situation created mass unsanitary conditions due to the arrival of lice which caused in due course an epidemic of Typhoid.

Greek Jews from Salonika originally settled in Stern camp. For some reason, they managed to get an occasional allocation of fresh milk, strictly for children, now and then, distributed by a Greek lady speaking French. My mother taught me to say, "*Un peu du lait s'il vous plaît,*" as I handed in my cup. I don't remember getting milk more than once.

US bombers flew in formation over our camp every day. We were told to stay inside to prevent us from seeing them. Nevertheless, we saw them passing by; we even had a strafing event now and then, and we rejoiced that our enemies were being bombed. After the planes had passed into the horizon, my friends and I looked to pick up the spent cartridges from the strafing. My mother didn't think it was a good idea to hoard them and arranged to dispose of them. Each time the bombers passed, I wondered whether the crew was eating cheese sandwiches. I figured that if I nevertheless went outside, they might drop a sandwich, knowing that I was very hungry. After the war, I heard that the crews of these bombers were icy cold up there, and no way they were eating on the flight to their destination. For a Dutch boy, a cheese sandwich was, under normal circumstances, a daily standard.

My father was in the men's barrack and worked across from the Stern gate at the Stern-designated kitchen. One day, he brought a packet of butter from that kitchen and was caught and punished for stealing it. He spent twenty-four hours in solitary confinement. The next morning, I waited for him at the gate, and an officer came and told me that my father was in good shape and on the way back to the Stern camp. Somehow, I think that they might have dealt easy with him.

My father was more than six feet tall. He wore a black leather coat, had blue eyes, and blond hair that was balding. I speculated that they dealt very easy with him because he might have spoken German with a true Bavarian accent. Anyhow, he didn't act nor look as if he had been punished.

Mother was in the female camp together with Erica and me. As in Westerbork, there was no schooling in Belsen. By now, I was eleven years old with nothing to do except to help carry the twice-daily fifty-liter thermos containers. Every day, we got fake hot coffee and a one-centimeter slice of brown bread in the morning, and in the evening back came the fifty-liter thermoses with a hot rutabaga (Swede) soup with some potatoes and carrots. I hated that soup, but I am sure my mother made me eat it.

Ernest and Erica visiting Bergen-Belsen
Memorial Site 2006.

4

THE LOST TRAIN

The Holocaust had a tough ending for us, as we were one of the three "lost" transports out of Belsen. On April 10, 1945, we were marched to the same rail track on which we had arrived, but this time a long line of cattle wagons awaited one thousand inmates to fill each cattle wagon with 100 inmates.

Hermann Goering somehow contacted and agreed with the 63rd Anti-Tank Regiment and the 11th Armored Division of the British Army to not engage in warfare when liberating Belsen on April 15, 1945. We were moved out of Belsen five days prior to the Brits arriving to liberate the camp. With a done deal, Goering ordered the Belsen commandant to lift 3,000 Jewish inmates out of Belsen for the simple purpose of making Belsen look less awful to the forthcoming British liberators. Nothing would/could ever make Belsen look good.

The reality is that the Brits were shocked to hell when they entered Belsen and saw that what they had liberated were mostly skeletons and dying bodies. Those that were alive needed immediate medical help in the sense of not overeating themselves off the Nazis' pile of hoarded, hard-to-digest food.

I learned years later that the three transports out of Belsen were intended to be rolled onto the bridges over the Elbe River near Berlin, which were due to be blown up to stop the approaching Russian armies from crossing them. We were in the lost transport for twelve days, and they were the worst days within all our three-and-a-half years of imprisonment in concentration camps.

By the time our transport reached the Berlin area, all the bridges had already been demolished.

The longer the lost train wandered around the limited available tracks, the more people died from either typhoid or hunger. My grandmother was in our wagon with end-of-life cancer, and she died. We sort of buried her in a bedsheet in a ditch along the track. My grandfather had already died in Belsen from a heart attack.

Our transport was stuck here and there, and our guards would then unlock the wagons' doors so that we could find water to drink and to wash ourselves. It was late at night, and we had nothing left to eat, and my mother sent Erica and me with a pot to beg for food at a farmhouse in the distance with a light in the window to show us the way to get there. When we rang the bell, the wife of the farmer appeared right away. She knew what we wanted, and she said that all she could spare were potato peelings. We gladly took them. Then we got back to the train.

We made a fire between two stones and cooked the peels until they were soft. We ate all the peels, and they tasted like potatoes, so we were glad to have had them. Many years later, I learned that the vitamins of a potato are hidden in the peels. Perhaps they saved us?

One day, our lost transport stopped at a railway station, and the guards allowed us out. My mother took me out and went to the opposite side, where a normal passenger train stood with Russian prisoners of war. She bartered a pack of cigarettes for a can of sardines, and that was my iron food reserve.

Once I was back in the cattle wagon, I was again shielded somehow by my mother. She helped me avoid seeing the worst of mankind within a cattle wagon, filled with starvation and disease.

Conditions within these wagons were beyond description, and being strafed by who knows who, surely by mistake, killed a woman in another wagon. Our train kept moving east, and within a few more days, the guards opened us up for the last time. Then they and the locomotive took off westward, and we were abandoned in a dense forest.

A few hours later, two Russian soldiers on horseback patrolling the track appeared, which confirmed that we could consider ourselves liberated. It was April 22, 1945. The end of WWII in Europe was official on May 8, 1945.

We learned about a farm beyond the forest. By then, my father and Erica were too sick with typhoid and stayed in the wagon. My mother and I walked to the village and found a parked tanker car at the village station. A closer look at the tanker showed a tag indicating it was full of condensed milk. My mother rushed me into the nearest vacant house, and we found two empty containers, which we filled with condensed milk. On the way back, we kept dipping our fingers into the condensed milk and thus got some good nutritious food. When we got back to our wagon, my father and Erica were too sick to eat.

The first thing that happened was that the Russians brought a few German women from another village, and they collected tables. We children were lifted onto the tables (we weighed mightily little), and the women washed us with soap and water and cut off all our hair to get rid of our lice. Then a Russian doctor ordered me to be sent to the field hospital, which happened to be a school. I had stopped eating, claiming that I wasn't hungry, but my mother knew that this was a symptom of starvation. She had a so-called iron food reserve—a can of Portuguese sardines, which she forced me to eat shortly before we were abandoned in the forest.

More than half of the 1,000 people on our lost transport died of either typhoid or starvation in Tröbitz, the farming village where we ended up.

They are buried, including my grandmother and all other victims who died during the train ride, at a Jewish cemetery in Tröbitz, which is most likely the only farm village in Germany with a Jewish cemetery.

My mother and I somehow were spared from the typhoid epidemic. At the hospital, I was fed rice soup with meat, which I liked, and when my mother came to fetch me, I shouted from the window what I had for breakfast! I was released from the field hospital the next day. My father and sister suffered from typhoid and hallucinated for several days in our temporarily borrowed home in Tröbitz. Then the disease tapered off slowly. We remained in the village for about two months, where we slept and ate food supplied by the Russian Army.

The Holocaust deprived me of normal nutrition for three-and-a-half years, between the ages of nine and twelve. Consequently, I had a growth disorder, which very gradually I never totally overcame.

In June 1945, the Russians had arranged for American trucks to pick us up from Tröbitz, and that was the beginning of our slow trip to Holland. But first, we had to travel through a lot of war-ravaged Germany.

The first sector of our trip out of Tröbitz brought us to Leipzig, which Allied bombers had totally burned down. Walking through the streets with rubble on both sides was a severe reminder that the bombers, which had flown so serenely over Belsen, may have brought this huge disaster to the inhabitants of Leipzig.

We exited the trucks; we had no baggage, and we walked into a kind of warehouse filled with mattresses.

I think my parents, without saying much, prepared us to not hate the Germans for what happened but to have pity on the survivors of Leipzig. During our first day walk through Leipzig, we came across a restaurant with a sign on the door that said: VERBOTEN FÜR DEUTSCHE (NO ACCESS FOR GERMANS). All four of us were stunned because we were reminded how that sounded when Jews were "verboten" to do this or that.

We had food coupons and German money from the Americans who brought us to Leipzig, and we entered the restaurant.

I don't remember whether we spoke German or Dutch, but judging how decimated our bodies looked and our worn clothing, the waiters must have been shocked enough to not question us. I only remember that the restaurants' meal was very frugal, but it didn't matter because it was a meal. I hope my father tipped the waiter.

At another place, my mother and I joined a queue, and a lady behind us said to my mother that my shoes were too worn out, and she would like to give me a pair of better ones from her son if I went with her to her apartment. So, I did. Walking onward, we passed an American facility with a black American guard. I had never seen a black person.

I got a better pair of shoes. When we got back to the queue, my mother thanked the lady profusely. This charitable moment in a destroyed Leipzig never left my memory. My family and I never turned harbored any hot hatred toward Germans because of the war. We silently only hated the German criminals, but not the general German public.

From Leipzig, we were transported in American-driven busses to Maastricht. That was our entry port into Holland. We were quarantined for two weeks, and we were registered as returning residents of Holland. Also, we received some Dutch cash, and the standard food coupons that were so desperately needed as all of Holland had starved the previous winter. All of Europe suffered from food shortages.

We paid, and we took the passenger train from Maastricht to Amsterdam in July 1945. When I stepped off the train onto the platform of the Amsterdam Central railway station, I finally fully grasped that all four of us had survived, which was a kind of miracle. The first week, we were guests of Dutch friends at their grand but totally ransacked apartment. Thereafter, we rented an apartment on the Overtoom, a busy street in Amsterdam. The flat required walking up a long wooden staircase.

I got to walk as part of a daily routine to and from my catch-up school. I passed in front of Vondelpark, where a

Coca-Cola vendor sold a bottle of this unique American drink. Naturally, I never ever heard of Coke, but I had some spending money, so I bought a bottle and drank it. The first bottle was definitely a hit. The following day, I bought it again, and the taste didn't repeat itself.

After having sampled two bottles of Coke, I never ever drank it again. Many years later, I learned that Coke was/is a very unhealthy, sugary drink and that by itself makes Coke and all pop drinks a no-no for me!

5

RECOVERING AFTER THE WAR

After the war, and when we were settled into a normal post-WWII life, nobody in our family ever touched on our concentration camp history. Somehow, we had a silent understanding, and that included my mother, father, and, eventually, my stepfather Jenö whenever I saw him. I can only assume that the Holocaust was such a terrible topic that nobody wanted to bring it up.

In 2013, UK Prime Minister David Cameron proposed building a Holocaust Memorial and a Learning Center near Westminster. But over the years, there were disputes about the location and cost, and the project stalled. It is finally expected to open in 2025. Part of the project called for 100 survivors to be interviewed so that their stories would be recorded and filmed for future generations. I was among them.

Natasha Kaplinsky, a famous ITV interviewer, was chosen to interview the survivors. When it was my turn, I told my story, and it was recorded and filmed. She was very encouraging and helped me talk about my camp and other Holocaust experiences.

I did this on a few occasions and learned, to my dismay, that while people were willing to listen, they had nothing to say when I finished my story. This left me with the impression that they either didn't care or weren't interested.

My sister Erica, once she retired from her Philadelphia high school teaching job, turned into a Holocaust speaker at the school district, and she also was asked to speak at synagogues and churches. Her prime message was that survivors must not hate German civilians but only those who were guilty and judged at the Nuremberg trials after the war.

It was only when we reached Amsterdam in July 1945 that I fully grasped that the war was over, that we had survived the Holocaust, and that all four of us could start a new life. My mother and sister went to the United States in 1946, the same year I was sent to a Swiss boarding school for boys to catch up on my education and regain my health.

Going to Switzerland meant I would travel on an airliner for the first time. My KLM flight was on a DC-3, and it was rather bumpy. Kloten Airport was tiny, and a relative was there to bring me to the Zurich Central Railway Station. From there, I took the train to St. Gallen. Waiting for me there was my new roommate, Warren

Smidt. We took a taxi to the *Institut auf dem Rosenberg*, which had a steep walkway I would get to know. But, on that day, the taxi drove us to the front of our house on the Rosenberg property.

Where you were housed depended on your age. Being amongst the youngest, Warren and I were placed in the Nussbaum house. I didn't have much luggage because I didn't have much clothing, so unpacking was easy. Warren then told me that he was part Swiss and part Dutch East Indies. I learned that he had spent the war in a Japanese concentration camp on Java in Dutch East Indian territory. I never met his parents, so I never knew who was Swiss and who was Dutch Indonesian. It didn't matter. Warren wasn't due to stay much longer in that boarding school, so I was on my own in that room for a while.

The classrooms we attended were all in the same house where we slept and washed. Washing meant sponging oneself in front of one of the several wash basins in warm water, and the teachers insisted that to finish the wash, it must be done with cold water. I never showered until I got to the United States. I don't remember my curriculum except that it covered a whole lot of subjects, and I just went with the flow in the German language. Gradually, I made friends. In my house was a Turkish boy, Saffet Bozkurt, with whom I got along very well. Also, there was a German boy about my age, Peter Gafgen, and Peter Singer, who was Austrian. The latter had an older brother in another house whose name was

Max Singer. I remained lifelong friends with Gafgen and Singer.

I gradually got to know a lot of the older boys in sports as well as in our woodworking class. I was told that there were thirty-eight different nationalities in that Swiss boarding school, of which I was perhaps the only stateless one. That's Switzerland for you in the sense that it welcomed strangers.

All meals were in a common large dining room sort of in the middle of all these houses, and two teachers always stood at the entrance to the dining room to inspect whether our hands were clean. We just presented our hands upward and then turned them inside to get past the teachers' inspection. I don't remember what we got for breakfast, lunch, or dinners, but even in Switzerland, which had not suffered during the war, short of food. So, we ate mostly frugal meals. However, compared to anything else I had eaten since 1941, it was all *wunderbar*! Because I was so undernourished, I was told to report every morning at 11 a.m. in the kitchen, where I would receive a thick slice of salami to boost my nutrition. I learned seventy-five years later that Pete Gafgen also ate that privileged salami slice. Whether that was a healthy snack can be debated!

At the entrance to the dining room stood a grand piano and, quite regularly, a talented pianist from the outside would play classical music for our pleasure while eating our dinner. For entertainment, we were taken on excursions. There were two destinations. One was to take the train to Rorschach on Lake Constance, where we could swim. The other was to walk up the Santis Mountain around St. Gallen. My shoes and clothing were inadequate for the mountain walk, so the wife of Dr. Lusser, a director of the school, took me by train to Zurich to shop at Jelmoli, and that is how I got my first new threads in five years, and a pair of shoes suitable for mountain walking. When I met Dr. Lusser himself, he sort of "blessed me" with a Swiss nickname: "Burstenbinder." It's hard to translate, but it implied that I was good at making "brushes." I had no idea how to make brushes, and I never even attempted that, but since that nickname was strictly between him and me, I didn't mind.

There was a cashier near the office of the management, where I signed for the outlays I needed, which my mother would settle. Also, from the start of my days at the school, I received five Swiss francs per month as pocket money. Just about $1.25 in 1946. We had some free daytime to go snack shopping in St. Gallen, and I liked this weekly chance to buy some Swiss chocolate, which was and still is world renowned because of the high-quality Swiss milk.

The daily activity at the Rosenberg was more than sufficient, meaning there was no boring moment. We were kept busy until bedtime. After lights out, if you were caught walking around the house, you would have to sit in your classroom and learn a poem by heart before the teacher would release you. It happened once because

Gafgen had organized a whole slew of boys to run around the house after lights. I was perhaps the only one caught; I wouldn't do that again!

I had acquired some French language in my Swiss School. Switzerland is split into three language zones—German (and Swiss German), French, and Italian. There is a fourth language, but only a tiny portion of the Swiss speak Romansh, a sort of Latin from people who settled in Switzerland around 500 years ago.

While at the Swiss boarding school, I received a letter from my mother in 1947 announcing that she had divorced my father in Mexico and married Eugene Por (nickname Jenö), whom she met in Westerbork. From Westerbork, Jenö endured Buchenwald and managed to survive.

Shortly after we settled in our own apartment in Amsterdam, Jenö Por visited with one red rose in his hand. He found us with the help of the Red Cross list of survivors. Jenö survived Buchenwald, and his Hungarian wife, Nelly, was sent to Ravensbruck, where she passed away shortly before liberation. So, looking backward, Jenö was keen on my mother from his days at her Westerbork barrack that she managed. Subsequently, my mother divorced Walter in Mexico in 1947, and later she was married to Jenö in America.

Hearing about the divorce via a letter from my mother didn't upset me; my mother praised Jenö, and I accepted her message that my future stepfather would be good to me.

My father wrote a lot of letters to my sister, Erica, in the United States, in which he expressed his regrets about the divorce. My father felt he had lost both his two semi-grown children. My mother's parents had tried feverishly to change my father's mind about settling in "neutral" Holland, and they figured that before the clock ran out, Walter should attempt to get American visas. Erich Gumperz, my mother Margot's brother, was already an American citizen in Vineland, New Jersey, and chances were that we might have received those visas before the war began.

Anyhow, I suspect that my father was stubborn and felt at home in Holland, and he was near his business associates in Zurich. A further cause of friction was that Walter and his brothers had declared bankruptcy in Munich; that business was known in Munich as Hesselberger & Herz, which manufactured male accessories. Margot's father was a wealthy industrialist and had sufficient funds to get us out of Europe to anywhere that would provide visas. Walter knew best; his business in Holland was recovering, and I presume that all these bits and pieces of stress were recalled by my mother after the war and made her more than ready to divorce Walter and marry Jenö.

Walter met a Christian lady at a dance in Amsterdam, and the two got engaged. Walter then invited Jenö and Margot to attend his Amsterdam wedding and they accepted because I think Jenö wanted to avoid bad feelings between them. In due course, Walter became a very successful sales agent for a big American hardware firm in Chicago, and they persuaded him to immigrate to Los Angeles, where he would be in charge of sales in California.

Unfortunately, Walter suffered from angina, and he died suddenly in Los Angeles of a heart attack on September 16, 1958, at age fifty-nine. I was in Lima, Peru, on business when Erica telegraphed the bad news to me. Erica attended the funeral; I was twenty-six years old and was busy in Lima and couldn't have reached the funeral in time.

The last time I saw my father was when he came to visit my New York City bachelor flat at 56 E. 89th St. and Madison Avenue. Our get-together was strained. At a certain moment, my father moved his right arm so quickly that I ducked to avoid a slap as if I was a child again. He had a history of slapping both Erica and me. Both of us were badly embarrassed, and we never met again and therefore never talked about it again.

Ernest, Margot, Walter and Erica Herz circa
1946.

The Netherlands 1946/47: from left to right:
Erica, Jenö, Marika, Margot, Ernest

Walter and Ernest, circa 1948

6

NAME CHANGE

I changed my name from Herz to Hilton in 1949 at age seventeen because that was the youngest age a US court allows for a name change. In the two prior years, while I attended a Quaker boarding school in Barnesville, Ohio, my classmates confused my Herz birth name with Hertz the car rental firm. They also rightly knew from my accent that I was German, and I was desperate not to be thought of as a German national for good reason.

Why was I in a hurry to change my name? By changing my name from Ernst Adolf Herz to Ernest Allen Hilton, I also shed all my years of Holocaust survival. Understand that I was born in the turmoil of Munich, Germany, in 1932 as Ernst Adolf Herz. My father told me years later that he insisted on that middle name because his father was Adolf Herz. The year 1933 was even more chaotic in German politics because President Paul von Hindenburg had died, and Adolf Hitler, who had joined the Nazi Party in 1919, was voted in as Germany's new chancellor and Führer of the Third Reich via a mostly ecstatic voting population. Hitler's first dictate as Führer was to denationalize all German Jews. That meant approximately 600,000 German Jews (about 0.75% of the German population) were now stateless in their country of birth.

My new name had implications. I didn't pretend that I was not Jewish if the question arose, but I realized that with Hilton as my surname, I very likely wouldn't be thought of as Jewish, so that was a calming consideration. I also grasped that for many people, I might be mistaken for a member of the Hilton Hotel chain. I never pretended that, but I knew that with that name, I might be assumed to be related. This quandary hit me in due course in terms of tipping. I was conscious that the Hilton name demanded a bit of extra tipping than I would have tipped as Herz.

After a while, I didn't worry about my new name because nothing unpleasant happened. On the contrary, I got better seating in a restaurant when I made a reservation in my name. When I checked in for flights—and I usually went first class—even then, I got the better first-class seats! On my flight on Swiss Air from Zurich to Bangkok, the attendant couldn't stop saying, "Mr. Hilton do you want this or that?" Or "What I can I do for you?" Only after a few hours of calm flying did it occur to me that she had a special pleasure to be in charge of my seat, and there was Mr. Hilton himself. I didn't respond very much, and probably that was the best way to deal with her enthusiasm.

So, when I changed my name from Herz to Hilton, I had effectively redefined myself as not being a Jew. Instead, I defined myself as Ernest A. Hilton.

It took a while for me to adjust to my new name. By that, I mean that by having exited from my Jewish name, I assumed theoretically to never again be abused as a Jew. Even if I accepted myself as a Jew, I didn't wear it on my sleeve. But if the question arose, I wouldn't cringe but answer that "yes, I am a Jew."

I also had worries about my Hilton name. I didn't like chauffeurs picking me up from LHR holding a sign saying "Hilton." I was definitely afraid that I might get kidnapped one day! Therefore, I ordered them to use "EAH" on the sign, which made me feel safer. I admit that it is quite likely that if I had kept my Herz name, I would very unlikely have encountered antisemitism because, until recently, the Holocaust sheltered Jews from abuse. The Hilton name shielded me sufficiently from antisemitism and generally provided me with a famously well-known name, which in a way supported me positively and psychologically.

One of my most memorable experiences as a result of my name change happened sixty-eight years later. While residing in London, I received a call from someone named James Hilton.

"Would you like to attend a Hilton family reunion?" he asked.

In all the years that I had carried the Hilton name, I never pretended to be a member of the Hilton Hotel chain. Consequently, I didn't hesitate to say, "I can't attend your reunion; I changed my name to Hilton."

His perfect response was, "You picked an honorable name."

I am very glad to admit that I was stunned by his response because it easily could have ended in an interrogation, if not potential abuse, for me having borrowed his name. Now I knew that I had truly chosen an honorable name that I had worn for sixty-eight years with a much better acceptance of my identity than when I was a Herz. With the name Hilton, nobody would assume that I was Jewish. That may explain why I never talked about my Holocaust experience because with the name Hilton, that doesn't make sense! I figured that irrespective of my new name, I was a Jew with a very long Jewish history, which ought to give me some pride rather than excuses. I also admired the State of Israel— not least because survivors of WWII settled there, and they helped make Israel into a thriving Jewish state.

The most common German surname, Muller (Miller), is shared by around 700,000 people. This is followed in popularity by the name Schmidt along with variants such as Schmitt or Schmitz (this comes from the blacksmith's trade), with Meier coming in third place.

Why did I choose Hilton? To start with, I had to keep the H in my surname because my grandfather owned and operated a silver-plating company under the brand name Hartmann Silver in Munich. When my mother, Margot Gumperz, married Walter Herz, her father, Benno Gumperz, showered the couple with every kind of silver-plated dinnerware and utensils engraved with the letter H. That was the fashion in the 1920s. The next obstacle was that I had three Herz uncles, of which one stayed Herz and moved to Johannesburg, South Africa, where he worked as a conductor at the Johannesburg Symphony Orchestra. Another immigrated to Southern Rhodesia (now Zimbabwe) and changed his name from Herz to Hurst. The third Herz changed his name from Herz to Hart and resided in St. Albans, UK. I didn't want to trespass on their turf. Instead, I was fascinated via the media by all the stories that Elizabeth Taylor was going to marry Nicky Hilton. Since I was a fan of Liz Taylor movies, I figured that it would be good also for my future wife to choose Hilton as my new surname. As it turned out, my first wife became Patricia Hilton Nossiter, with no offspring, and whom I divorced after sixteen years of marriage. My second wife is Saisampan Hilton Suvarnapradip. She's a Thai national, and we had a son named Benno Baramee Hilton, born in London in 1981.

When I started to travel on business, I had a business card, so there was no question as to my new name. The only question, which occurred quite often when I checked in at a Hilton Hotel, was, "Are you family?" I interpreted that as being a family member of the Hilton Hotel chain. Perhaps I would have had a discount if I had affirmed that question, but I never did that. Instead, I had a pat answer: "Not yet!" The clerk didn't know what to say about that response, so that ended my registration, and I was satisfied to be on my way to my room, which was always neat and spacious, and the hotel itself was somehow more social than any other hotels I frequented.

Very many years later, when I resided in London with Saisampan and Benno, we were recommended to spend a summer holiday at Forte Dei Marmi on the Italian Riviera. While I had sold my New York condo, my wife owned a fabulous co-op apartment at the Campanile Building at 450 E 52nd St. When we moved to London, she rented her co-op to an Italian CEO and wife, and they were delighted to have this temporary luxury New York home overlooking the East River and the garden of the Rothschilds (not the bankers) one floor below us.

When we seriously contemplated a Forte Dei Marmi holiday Saisampan, called this CEO and requested that he introduce us to a property agent in Forte Dei Marmi because we wanted to rent a vacation house for six weeks. I presumed he handled that request easily via his office in Rome because he answered promptly with the name, address, and phone number of the recommended Forte Property Agency. What we couldn't have known at the time was that the CEO might have assumed that, based on the luxury location of his NYC rental flat and

Saisampan's surname of Hilton, I was very likely a member of the hotel chain.

I drove from London to Forte Dei Marmi. When we arrived, we found the gents' office, and he arranged a house-looking tour for us. The first house we saw was facing the sea and looked sort of like a miniature castle. I immediately fell for it, and he told us that it was rented, but he would see what could be done. The next day, we saw the premises and learned that an Italian artist had rented some space in the mini-castle, but there was plenty of space for us and our nanny and Benno once they arrived via a flight from London to Pisa airport.

After we spent a few days at the mini-castle and got friendly with the artist, it occurred to me that while we had a nice view of the beach and the Mediterranean, the highway along the sea was quite noisy. The agent immediately suggested we get a house inland, which would not be noisy at all, and we could easily rent bikes to move around Forte. The house we ended up renting was in a very nice large garden, and we fell in love with Forte and that property. We rented it for our six-week summer holiday and invited friends.

One day, our property agent came and asked whether I would kindly meet a few architects from Genoa who wished to invite the Hiltons for dinner in Forte and discuss the opportunity to have the Hilton chain build a hotel in Genoa? Saisampan was flabbergasted, but I immediately assumed that the CEO had indeed assumed that I was from the Hilton Hotel chain, so I was in a big quandary. If I were to explain that I had changed my name for my benefit, the CEO would be stuck with having promoted me erroneously, and it would backfire badly on him. So, the only way not to rock the boat. I had to play the role in such a way that nobody could be hurt. It so happened that the restaurant chosen was by now our favorite in Forte, so I kept telling Saisampan that I would deal with it, and she could just enjoy the dinner.

The three architects drove three hours to Forte. The maître d' knew us and seated us majestically with the architects. We mutually introduced ourselves, but I didn't present a business card (because I didn't have one with "Hotel" on it), and thank goodness, neither did they. The architects did most of the talking, which boiled down to I would promote their wish to build a Hilton Hotel in Genoa. All I did was say that I thought it was a good idea, that Genoa was a fast-growing port city and that I would pass the word to the people who would decide on such a project.

This was encouraging enough, and the dinner was a sort of success for the architects, and we were relieved when they said goodbye, and we thanked them for the invitation. Saisampan hadn't said a word; I was pleased that they were perhaps sufficiently satisfied with my optimistic commentaries because nobody could agree to such a project over a dinner invitation.

A few days later, the agent came again and told me that the most famous yacht builder in Viareggio, who resides in a mansion in Forte, had asked him to invite us for dinner at his home. This even made me feel more embarrassed, but I had played along once, so I must do it again. We arrived on time at the mansion and the dining room was splendidly laid out, and two waiters were in attendance. After a lot of small talk, the owner came to the point. He said that if the Hiltons would like to have a luxury yacht, he would build them the most fantastic model, and could I help him bring this to reality? I said the same sort of thing, that it was a great idea but that I could only propose it and a decision would take time. Subsequently, I learned that Viareggio is where about a fifth of these gigantic elite boats are constructed.

Once again, Saisampan said nothing, nor did she admire my play-acting. By now, I felt like a real intermediary, although I didn't even know where in the United States the Hilton chain headquarters were located, nor how far that would be from the nearest yacht port. The end of this drama was that the agent came a third time to say that he would drive me up to the most important marble mine in the mountains overlooking Forte. The owner of the mine awaited me. His request was that if the Hilton Hotel chain went ahead and built a hotel in Genoa, could I please put a few good words for marble to be purchased from his famous mine? I reassured him that I would do that because it makes a lot of good sense. But it might take a while before the decision is made to go ahead in Genoa.

So, that was short and sweet, and I had done my duty to the Italian CEO to play the part of a "real" Hilton. I saved not only his face but also the agent's face. While Saiampan and I were on the way back to London from Galileo Galilei Airport in Pisa and walking toward immigration checkout when the property agent stood behind us, and he shouted to the immigration officer while pointing his finger at us, "ALBERGO HILTON!" I know enough Italian to get it: he was making sure that the Hiltons of the Hilton chain were getting VIP treatment while departing Italy. The immigration officer didn't say anything but stamped my US passport, which showed the secret I didn't like, that I was born in Germany.

Funnily, it never occurred to me to somehow get in touch with the Hilton Hotel and clue them in on the potential hotel investment in Genoa. Even if I had the courage to explain this situation to a Hilton executive, I had no business cards from the three applicants, so my message would have rung even worse than it was. Had these "promoters" asked for my business card, I was ready to explain (more like circumvent) that in America, we don't take our business cards on vacation! Not a strong excuse because if I were legit, I would have the details of my business card in my head, but there wasn't any Hilton Hotel data up there.

This event took place in the early 1980s, so by now, it is nothing but a fun anecdote, and at least I know that four Hilton properties already operate in Genoa. Probably, all due to me because the architects liked my upbeat responses to their vision. I am not sorry about all that bluffing I engaged in, but nobody got hurt while I was pretending to be useful to the executives at McLean, Virginia, and the Italian entrepreneurs! And, to end this story, all the minor actors in this affair never realized that they were blowing their horn to the wrong Hilton.

7

UNIVERSITY AND LEARNING A TRADE

After a year at the Swiss school in St. Gallen, I received a US immigration visa. With that on hand, I returned to Holland and spent two weeks with my father and his wife-to-be prior to boarding an 8,000-ton American freighter that was converted to carry military personnel. I slept in a hammock for ten days while traveling alone. I was under the care of the captain because I was not quite fifteen years of age.

When I disembarked in August 1947 at the Port of Philadelphia, I was met by my mother and sister Erica. Little did I know that two weeks later, I would be traveling on the Pennsylvania Railroad via Pittsburgh to Wheeling, West Virginia. From there, I took a taxi to Olney, the Quaker boarding school in Barnesville, Ohio. This choice was made by my Uncle Eric (my mother's brother), who figured that since I did not yet speak a lot of English, I would feel better at a small boarding school with a maximum of 100 students instead of attending a crowded public high school.

Olney certainly was a very different kind of school—more so because it was "ancient" in the sense that we spoke to each other with "thee or thou" in honor of George Fox, the founder of Quakerism. Unsurprisingly, Olney was very different than the institute in St. Gallen, but I managed to pick up the English language quite rapidly. And I liked the farm attached to the school where we grew most of our food. Since we grew a lot of apples, we were served applesauce with each meal. (I forgot to ask them to serve potato pancakes with all that applesauce). The idea was to take a slice of dark bread soaked in fat-free milk and a good helping of applesauce on top. I like it a lot.

There were only two dorms—one for boys and one for girls. So that, too, was quite a different environment. In my Swiss boarding school, there were only boys. There were no excursions, but we could go to the movies in Barnesville. I also liked that after hours, our teacher would drive to the nearby gas station and buy pints of ice cream for those who wanted it and had the 25 cents to get it hauled back to the dorm.

One afternoon, I was asked to join a bunch of boys working on a neighbor's farm, removing tree trunks from the earth to make space for plowing. This was hard work. When done, the farmer paid each one of us 10 cents. I knew enough to think about how poor the farmer was. I am still ashamed that in America, labor was paid so low because the farmer couldn't afford to pay more.

At Olney, there were three subjects I particularly cherished: public speaking, touch typing, and a requirement that I read one book a week and write book reports on each. To get to know the girls, we were allowed to have a weekly early-evening moonlight walk on our large property, holding hands. This was a very new experience for me, too, although it wasn't meant to be romantic. We did have girlfriends with whom we exchanged very neatly folded little messages of proper content only. Ardith Hall was my girlfriend, and she even arranged for me to go with her to her home for Thanksgiving. Despite feeling comfortable at Olney, I enjoyed going back to Manhattan for Christmas because Jenö's brother Fred and his wife, Zina, and daughter Susan provided a great Christmas party/dinner at their home with loads of presents in their flat on East 96th Street.

After I graduated (by mistake) a year too soon from the Quaker boarding school, Jenö invited me for a three-week holiday in Paris. Jenö had family members with children my age in Paris, where I would be lodged. The French family apartment was more than 400 years old; it was near Cluny and close to Rue du Chat-qui-Pêche, the narrowest street in Paris! I was lodged in a kind of tiny pentagon-shaped space. I had to walk through all the other bedrooms to get to the single bathroom.

I slept very well, so that wasn't an issue. In 1949 the food situation in France was almost as bad as it was elsewhere in Europe, so we never ate at a restaurant; we only ate at home, and baguettes were off the table as too expensive. We ate bread from big loaves. Every day I was given a note with my cultural destination for the day. I don't recall how I managed to get home every afternoon, but I did. I became, and remain, a Francophile. On the last night in Paris, the family invited me to a cabaret near their apartment, and we ate well and drank wine. I had been so keen to drink red wine for weeks, so that was my farewell event—to finally sip wine.

I spent the next two years at the University of Maine. Why there? At that time, it was the only college in the United States that offered a degree in paper and pulp technology. I was destined to work in that industry because my Hungarian stepfather, Jenö, was a partner in such a firm. When I started at the University of Maine, which was a 500-mile car drive from Great Neck, I was overwhelmed with new subjects such as chemistry (I didn't even know what that word meant). English grammar was like a thunderclap for me to catch up on. My freshman year was almost totally nonstop chaos.

My sophomore year was better because I transferred from a dorm to a fraternity. Before I was going to be hazed, Ted Gross saved me from this activity, and I am still thankful for his intervention. On the other hand, I learned to play poker and drink whiskey. But, in the two years at Maine, I never had even an inkling of a girlfriend. On the other hand, the frat house had a good cook, and I learned to eat peanut butter and jam sandwiches when hungry—pretty good except for the white bread, which I considered unhealthy.

My classwork was no longer overwhelming, and I had already worked one summer vacation at a paper mill in Lawrence, Massachusetts.

The following year, I had to attend a summer course at Hofstra College to redo a bloody chemistry course. I finally passed it! Then, I was due to spend the rest of the summer at a paperboard mill—Container Corp. of America, in the Manayunk neighborhood of Philadelphia. When that was done, my time at the University of Maine was finished.

The other two years were spent at Columbia University, where I majored in economics. Going to school in Manhattan was already a big social step upward vs. the two years of no social contacts to speak of in Maine. My junior year at Columbia University was spent at Furnald Hall with Stanley Harris as my roommate, who was taking a law degree. The economics teacher was my first instructor with whom I had the pleasure of really learning something. I had very few friends since I spent the day at Jenö's office in the sample room because it makes the paper industry tick.

I took my courses, including Spanish language, in the late afternoon, and therefore there was no time to socialize. In my senior year, socializing became better. I was able to rent a three-bedroom apartment close to the Hudson River and within walking distance of Columbia University. Rather surprisingly, a girl from the University of Maine was my first girlfriend. I don't know what she was studying, but she was a nice friend. Two other students paid their share of the rent and used the flat, so we were a congenial little group.

I graduated from Columbia in 1954 with a BS in economics and moved into a bachelor apartment at 56 East 89th Street off Madison Avenue. It happened to be available because Jenö and partners owned the building. From then on, I worked all day long at American Paper & Pulp Co. at 23rd Street and Fourth Avenue.

From 1955 on, my career expanded quickly. My first overseas experience was spending three months in the Vienna office, where the business was started in the 1920s as Molnar & Greiner in Vienna. The paper industry in Austria is quite big, so I was sent to a variety of different paper mills to learn how they operated and how we would export their paper assortments to worldwide customers. At the time I was in Vienna, it was still occupied by the four Allied victors of WWII. A famous movie comes from that era was *Four in a Jeep*, about American, British, Russian, and French soldiers.

The charm of Vienna was again alive, and the opera and symphony orchestras were in full swing—especially famous on New Year's Day when it was broadcast worldwide. Both Jenö and Fred were frequent visitors to the M&G office, and they had a flat in Vienna so that they could bring their wives along. I had a room at a boarding house, which was good enough for me. On the outskirts of Vienna is the so-called Heurigen, where one goes to drink too much fresh wine and eat grilled chicken and sing Viennese songs. I enjoyed these outings and, of course, ended up tipsy. On the way back to Vienna, we would stop at a restaurant and eat either chicken or goulash soup, which would sober us up in time for the next morning.

I spent time learning the paper trade in NYC, Vienna, Copenhagen, Denmark, Sarpsborg, Norway, and Johannesburg, South Africa, then returned to Manhattan. In Sarpsborg, I was introduced to the CEO of Borregaard, a chemical company. I also met a very jovial Norwegian girl called Elsa, and she turned out to become the wife of Leo Braun, the only son of Gustav Braun and his wife in Copenhagen, with whom I transacted a lot of business.

From 1958 to 1960, I worked in Bogota and, from there, traveled the rest of South America (except Argentina and Brazil). During that period in South America, I became pretty fluent in the Spanish language. After two years in Bogota, I was recruited by Bunzl Pulp & Paper Ltd. in London. With the blessing of my stepfather and his partners, they urged me to accept the Bunzl offer because all of them were ready to retire.

After two years of working and enjoying London, I wished to return to Manhattan. By coincidence, Bunzl had an international trading corporation in NYC, and the president was due to retire within six months, and I could take over that position. Perfect.

8

_____

SOUTH AMERICA

When I was an intern, I was paid a weekly salary of $50, which, allowing for inflation, is $492.54 a week in 2021. My flat on 89th Street was rent-controlled, so whatever the rent was, I could afford it. The flat was rather dark because its location was facing the rear of the building, but it didn't bother me, as I only needed it to sleep in. I continued to work in the sample room.

The paper export business needs a whole array of all kinds of different qualities of paper so that when we get an inquiry, for example, for an order of 100 reams at 100 sheets at 22x34" of white onionskin paper (also available in many colors), we would airmail the sample of onionskin we could supply as well as the price per ream. Onionskin was the name of very thin paper used for making more than one copy of a typewritten letter using carbon paper. In those days, we used the standard paper industry codebook to communicate with our agents. That codebook wasn't to hide secret info; it was made to save money by reducing the number of characters in a telegram. So, instead of telegraphing, "We offer 100 reams of onionskin at $22/ream FOB NY Port (free on board) or CIF Barranquilla (cost, insurance, and freight), the code for the FOB price could have been ERLZA, whereas the CIF code would be ERLQB. I learned to not only write code but also translate incoming code into English. The codebook was not only hefty, it was sort of the size of the first printed Gutenberg Bible. So, this is how we communicated worldwide with our agents, who were the middlemen between the ultimate buyer and our office in NYC. The agents' sales commission was set at 3 percent on the FOB (free on board) value.

Within the partnership of American Paper & Pulp Co. Inc. was the original pioneer Adalbert Greiner, who fled Austria in time to evade WWII. He went from Vienna to NYC and temporarily lost his Molnar & Greiner firm in Vienna to the Nazis. Greiner re-established the business in NYC. He owned the largest number of shares of the private company and therefore had the nicest office. When he saw me occasionally, he would jovially ask, "Have you earned a dollar today?" I felt sort of like Dagwood from the cartoons! Well, I wasn't as yet making money for the firm, but my time would come.

There is a funny anecdote about Mr. Greiner's earliest experiences in buying paper for export from an American paper mill. On this occasion, he negotiated a big deal with the mill owner himself, and when all the details were settled, the owner asked, "How are you going to pay me, Mr. Greiner?"

Mr. Greiner responded, "As usual, I pay via a confirmed irrevocable letter of credit."

Well, the mill owner, doing business only within the United States, looked askew at Mr. Greiner and replied, "Mr. Greiner, with or without a letter of credit, we can't do business."

I suppose Mr. Greiner had an internal laugh, but he then clued the mill owner, and he called in his CFO, and all was in butter, as they say in Vienna.

So, business had its funny sides as well.

Meanwhile, I graduated from the sample room to writing letters in response to daily inquiries. The person who was my mentor in getting the hang of composing business letters was Tom Greiner, Mr. Adalbert Greiner's son, who had spent most of his career up to then at our paper wholesale business in Shanghai, where Fred Por (Jenö's younger brother) was in charge. In those days of long-distance travel, there were no flights. Fred Por, who also started his career at Molnar & Greiner Vienna, traveled to Shanghai on a Lloyd Trestino passenger ship, which took six weeks from Trieste to Shanghai.

He resided in the French section of Shanghai, which I visited once and found to be still in very good condition. Fred also got married in Shanghai to a White (as opposed to Red) refugee from Russia named Zinaida, whose name was shortened to Zina. In due course, Susanne Por was born in Shanghai and grew up in time to get to know Tom Greiner.

My letter writing improved from year to year, but even more to the point, I gradually got to understand that our first competitor abroad wasn't only another paper exporter from, say, Scandinavia, but the sales capability of our agents. Sales agents abroad would take on whichever line of business they felt they could handle. In other words, they knew too little about each product line but probably enough that they made their best sales on one or two lines of goods that they understood and thus earned an income from. Paper wasn't one of those easy sales because it was a complex line of business. I came to the conclusion that irrespective of all the samples we submitted and all the telegrams we sent to our agents with explanations, our turnover in Latin America was weak. Consequently, I explained to the partners my intent to be the Latin American sales manager working out of the headquarters in Bogota and regularly visit our South American agents to support their sales efforts. They agreed, except that I should stay away from Rio de Janeiro and Buenos Aires because we had such good agents in those countries. My salary was raised to $100 a week, with all expenses such as rent, flights, taxis, etc. reimbursed monthly.

Moreover, to provide me with a monetary incentive, I was promised an overriding commission on all Latin American sales at a .05 percent commission, whereas the agents would continue to receive their usual 3 percent.

Since sales ran around an average of $2500/order so this small commission added to the incentive.

I chose South America because I had two years of Spanish language at Columbia, so I wouldn't be speechless! Without much ado, I gave up my bachelor's flat, and I flew on Avianca to Bogota and into the unknown. The first step was to settle down in a boarding house, which was a cinch. Within a few weeks, I was very friendly with a guy from Cali who looked after rubber wheels sales for Goodyear and Jorge, another simpatico guy from San Jose, the capital of Costa Rica. I don't know what his line of business was. Jorge proposed that the three of us rent a house, get a cook and a cleaning lady, and our living expenses would be lower and our comfort better. I immediately agreed. A few days later, we were installed in a nice district of Bogota with a bus stop nearby. The cook and the cleaning lady were in their respective jobs! I am talking about 1958 when I landed in Bogota, and I was twenty-five years old.

Unbeknownst to me, the local habit was to go home for lunch, have a half-hour Siesta, and then go back by bus to the office. A few days into that routine, Jorge came into my bedroom, saw me reading the newspaper, and told me very precisely that reading after lunch was unhealthy and that I ought to sleep. This advice is even good nowadays but going home to have lunch seems to have totally disappeared even in South America.

Another side effect of this lunch at home was that my local agents, Mr. Asch with wife and partner Mr. Froehlich, invited me quite often to their home for lunch. Since they were all Viennese, the menu was superb, and the local Bavarian German-brewed beer was the prime beer in Colombia. So as love goes through the stomach, I was very happy to see them regularly and enjoy their cuisine. I don't think I napped at their home, but it is likely that I did so on their living-room couch while they went upstairs to their bedrooms.

Every day my Spanish language improved because Mr. Froehlich introduced me to old and new customers, so that was a good beginning. And when new inquiries originated, the agents would have me deal with the new customer right away. So gradually, our range of Bogota customers grew.

I don't know how the following social event happened, but one early evening a neighbor who was Mexican and represented a Mexican pharmaceutical company in Bogota came to our house with three young ladies. Roberto, one could see right away, was a lady's man. After small talk, he said that he brought these three friends because they don't have boyfriends, and they asked him to help them find boyfriends. Exactly his style! Thus, I got "matched" to a tall lady who Roberto said was "suitable for you, Ernesto." I said "okay," and *si mucho gracias,* and was introduced to Offie. Her real name was Ophelia, a divorced wife with two young daughters and a father who was a retired Japanese ambassador to

Colombia, whom I would never meet. I was quite surprised to be linked with a Japanese girlfriend, but it happened to work out very well.

The other chaps got their allotted girlfriends, so Roberto had done his job and left us. Offie spoke good English, but I think I spoke as much Spanish as I could to increase my vocabulary. None of the girls slept with us in our house—at least not Offie. She had a secret discreet tryst place of her own, and we would smooch there! When she would be in the mood, she would fetch me in her car.

Since I only used Bogota as my headquarters, I was away from there for two or three weeks at a time to visit the rest of South America. Our German agent in Caracas was a very astute sales agent, so I didn't spend much time there. On one occasion, a Caracas customer requested that I get him a new air conditioner for his Cadillac. I immediately volunteered. I alerted NYC to buy and pay for the air conditioner so that I could fly to Detroit to pick it up and bring it back to Caracas. There was no DHL in those days. It worked like clockwork, and the next day I brought the new a/c to the customer, who was definitely grateful.

At one of those Caracas visits, my agent urged me to enjoy the annual carnival in Port of Spain, Trinidad. Since the direct flights were sold out, I had to fly via a rural Venezuelan airport from where I could reach Port of Spain. The first thing was to get a bed, and I got that done at a kind of barrack facility in Port of Spain for men only. The next morning, I joined the "jump up" parade accompanied by empty oil barrels suitable for drumming. They made a terrific rhythmic sound. We walked or jumped through town with plenty of rum to drink, and it was a really unique kind of street party. In the evening, I bought a ticket at the best hotel in town to enjoy a buffet and more music. It was probably the most unique event I participated in during my two years in Latin America.

Then it was back to Caracas to get to Ecuador, which for business reasons involved both Quito and Guayaquil, the two most active cities. The simple potato came from South America, but the best potatoes in the world grow in Ecuador. It was a real treat to consume these local potatoes in their various Ecuadorian recipes. Quito is a tourist paradise as it is all about the Spanish era and a chance to stand on the equator. The Quito airport was akin to Hong Kong's old airport in that we flew between a narrow mountain pass into the landing strip, which is similar to the old days in Hong Kong, except instead of mountains, there were skyscrapers to fly in between until landing.

Our Quito agent was also German, and again he was very clued in to the local customers. Still, I walked through Quito to visit these buyers and could persuade them to add new qualities of paper to their wholesale paper businesses. I found Guayaquil more enchanting than Quito, perhaps because Harry Belafonte had made the "Banana Boat Song (Day-O)" so popular. I used to go to the harbor and watch the loading of the banana boats in the cool of the evening, and it was all handled by male labor who didn't sing. Not only were the bananas going onboard, but lots of big rats went there as well. An oddity in Guayaquil was that to buy postage stamps, instead of buying them in the post office, there were postage vendors outside the post office who sold the same stamps at a small discount. I never came across that elsewhere.

So, Guayaquil on the Pacific Ocean was a busy Port. Quito is at a much higher altitude than Bogota, but neither level bothered me. Nevertheless, it was nice to be at sea level when I flew to Peru on a PANAGRA jet (stands for Pan Am + Grace, the shipping company at the time) and landed at the Peruvian International airport at Callao, the Port of Lima. Lima is a fantastic capital city, and I enjoyed the hotel I used because it was opposite the Swiss Inn, where I ate traditional Swiss cuisine at times. Peruvian cuisine was even more attractive, especially ceviche of shrimp plus Peruvian pisco sour cocktails.

One evening, when I exited the Swiss Inn, a nice Peruvian girl about my age grabbed me by the hand unexpectedly, and she walked me to her place where I slept that night. In France, there is a little drawing of a girl like the Peruvian who grabs a man and, running along with him, says, *Fais moi plaisir*, which translates into "Give me pleasure."

The next morning, I took her to a private beach near Callao. Our Lima agent was of British origin and so we could work together very well. In those days, agents often arranged a rendezvous with a girl for the benefit of the visitor. There was not much discussion, nor did I have to pay anything, so I chalked it up as a goodwill gesture. On another visit to Lima, a European man approached me and said that he was a messenger from a single German woman and she would like to meet me. I said okay, and a while later, she came. She looked nice and took me in her car for a ride to the beach, where we parked, and we kissed for a while. Then she drove me to her house, where I learned the concept of her intent which was *Fais moi Plaisir,* although she didn't say that, but that was her intent and need, and I was very happy to comply. I stayed until she drove me back to my house! It turned out she, too, was a divorcee, and I met her almost every time I was in Lima, and she would take me for excursions around the area. Some years later, when I worked in London, she invited me to a very chic luncheon party on Church Street, Hampstead, near where I had my flat. Then we lost track of one another.

Contrary to what I said about the usage of letters of credit, we would forego an l/c if the value of an order were too small. In Lima, we supplied colored envelope paper to a small shop that operated an envelope-making machine run by a mature German man who worked the machine together with his grownup daughter. I twice visited them to request that they pay the overdue bank draft. The third time the daughter told me that her father had committed suicide. Neither the father nor the daughter ever explained why their business was failing. I don't remember the amount due, but it was perhaps around $500, which was a small sum. I assumed that the suicide story was real, and I felt very badly that someone would die for being unable to pay such a modest sum. I even speculated that the German might have been a Nazi now residing in Peru for his own private reasons.

Even now, sixty-three years later, I feel very badly and wonder if the suicide was true or if it was only a trick to get out of debt. It's not because I would even bother her for that old debt., but I wish to know that her father didn't commit suicide since that has bothered me over all these years! I would like to know that he had a better life once I no longer pressed for the debt payment and that he and his daughter made a success from their envelope production business.

When I visited all our customers in Lima with our agent, I flew to La Paz, Bolivia, where the airport is at 12,000 feet. My agent was a Swiss man used to mountains and was very fit. So, I had to walk up and down the hilly streets of La Paz carrying my heavy briefcase of paper samples. He had no mercy, so I just managed it. I was very impressed with the unique dresses and hats of the Bolivian indigenous women. As this route became routine, I also used the opportunity to once cross Lake Titicaca on a Scottish reassembled ferryboat from Puno in Peru to Copacabana in Bolivia, which took a whole night. Since the crossing from Puña starts early evening, we didn't get much viewing of this famous lake at a height of 12,507 feet (3,812 meters) in the Andean Altiplano, the highest and the largest lake in the world with a catchment area of 58,000 kilometers.

I did see a few unique local reed canoes on that lake. My single cabin on board was tight. We were only a few businesspeople on that crossing. I recall vividly that there were two Frenchmen with me at the dining table, and when the Jell-O dessert arrived, they kept looking at it as if it were oddities (they were to them), and they shook the plate to make the Jell-O shake so that they could laugh at that dessert. Seemingly Jell-O hadn't reached France as yet. I don't remember whether they gathered their courage and ate it anyhow. The next morning, I arrived at the Port of Copacabana, Bolivia, from where I took a grand viewing of the Bolivian countryside via a steam locomotive train ride to La Paz.

I didn't go to Chile for reasons I don't know, although much later, when I sold cigarette filters, I did get to do filter business in Chile and I landed in Santiago for a night and day and the following day flew to Antofagasta, the second largest city of Chile, where British American Tobacco operated a cigarette factory. Antofagasta is worth remembering for its fantastic seafood from the Pacific Ocean. Next was Asuncion, the capital of Paraguay, but no cigarette factory. After that, I visited Montevideo, the capital of Uruguay, and there, too, was no cigarette factory but instead twelve famous beaches along the Atlantic Ocean, which were mostly visited for a holiday by Argentinians.

Ernest and Roberto Erdos taking a Sunday
stroll in Bogotá. Feb 1959.

Ernest's membership of the Aeroclub de
Colombia from 1961

9

NEW JOB, NEW TRAVELS

In the two years that I worked in and from Bogota, I enjoyed one hobby and took one vacation with Offie, my Japanese girlfriend. That was from early 1960. My hobby was that I took flying lessons on a Piper Cub plane at a small airport with a flight instructor who happened to be the private pilot of Gustavo Rojas Pinilla, the president of Colombia at that time.

Offie drove me to the airport and waited in the coffee shop for me to return. I didn't have a knack for flying a plane, and when the instructor started some acrobatic flying, I got seasick and called it quits, which was a bad decision since rolling around in the sky wasn't my purpose. By then, I could lift off by myself and land by myself (with the captain seated behind me), so I wasn't a complete dud anyhow.

I took a vacation with Offie at Cartagena, located along the Caribbean Sea. We stayed at a nice hotel with a grand garden, and we splashed in the sea. We also played tourist and went to the museum home of Simón Bolívar, the liberator of South America who fell from grace toward the end of his fight to liberate South America from Spain.

About two years into my stint in Latin American sales management, I received a telegram from Bunzl in the UK, which was a big competitor of ours. The CEO of the paper export department, George Seton, would like to talk to me and he gave a date when he would come to see me. Seton asked me to join Bunzl Paper & Pulp and move to London. I realized that during those two years in Bogota, I had cut into their turnover in Latin America, so the best way to reverse the damage was to hire me. We didn't even talk about salary, but I did say that I was interested but needed to consult the owners of American Paper & Pulp in NYC.

This he accepted, and I would cable him with my answer within two weeks.

Before I quit Bogota, a very big customer of ours, Sami Rohr, also had a project for me to consider. The Llanos of Colombia is an area similar to the Pampas in Argentina. He was considering establishing a family ranch with a huge agricultural land area for his pleasure and business, and he wanted me, along with one of his staff, to fly into that area and spend time looking around for a suitable location to build such a property where I would be the manager. I agreed, and the survey we made took three days. The staff member, the pilot, and I flew across the mountains facing Bogota and gradually found the strip of land where a local guide with three horses was awaiting us. The landing on grass was quite smooth, and we disembarked. After small talk, we all were astride our horses, and off we went. I don't know what I was looking at, but it was certainly an empty vista for miles. So, to build a homestead with no neighbors anywhere in the middle of this empty territory might have been a good investment, but I couldn't see myself managing a void. We slept two nights near a waterfall, which we used as our daily shower, and we ate over a fire and cooked locally shot meat. I quite enjoyed the cowboy style and easy horse riding, but I was still a city boy. On the third day, the plane fetched us, and back we were in Bogota about an hour later.

Rohr understood my negative response. He had made his first fortune in the wholesale button trade. He then expanded into wholesale paper selling, and we served him well. He did, much later, invest in the Llanos and operated a huge farm, which made him a multimillionaire, but he and his family moved to Miami, but I never met him again.

Meanwhile, in 1960, I had spoken to Jenö, and the partners' answer was that all of them were about to retire and that Tom Greiner had found a new business for himself as the American Agent for Jagenberg AG, a German precision paper slitting machinery business he could manage on his own. So, there was no choice but to move to London and work for Bunzl. Little did I know that I would work for them for the next twenty years, mostly from NYC but twice for short spells in London.

In due course, I landed in London in the summer of 1960 and started what would be a two-year stint at Bunzl doing the same business as I had done for American Paper & Pulp in NYC. On my first day at Bunzl, Seton introduced me to Hugo Bunzl. He was quite aged and knew Adalbert Greiner from Vienna prior to WWII. He looked me over and then told Seton that he considered me family and therefore agreed with me joining his firm. Except, and this was the reason that I only stayed two years in London, the British business style was considerably different than what I had absorbed in NYC, let alone being in charge on my own in South America! Some aspects of British business style were useful. Otherwise, I found that we talked the talk instead of doing the transactions. I gradually got the hang of it, but I missed the business style I had developed while working in South America, meaning I was locked down at Friendly House, the headquarters of Bunzl. As usual, I started my home in London at a boarding house in Belsize Park. Now I learned to bathe in a tub instead of a shower, which I had in NYC, in Bogota, and in all the hotels I used in South America. The breakfast at the boarding house was so-so, and I never met any other boarder. So, Seton helped me, and I found a very pleasant bachelor flat on Reddington Road not far from Hampstead tube station. The same flat that I had at the top of the house had a twin across the landing, where a dentist about my age,

Mike Abrahamson, resided. The landlord was named Felix.

One evening, Mike returned to his flat with two Australian girls who had either "engaged him," or he had made a go for them. Either way, the one that he liked went to his flat, leaving me with the other named Patti, who, without any hesitation, crawled into my bed, where she chatted me up. At that stage, it was commonly accepted that Australian girls went on UK visits primarily to find a husband. I was thirty years old, and I was hopelessly looking for a wife.

Mike Abrahams, a dentist professionally, was a good mate, and we often spent our free time together. Mike was from Grimsby, and he drove me there once, which enabled me to see the famous and huge fish market. The boarding house we stayed in overnight was quite nice, and gradually, I got the sense of what being British means besides a good cup of tea! For sure, the pub plays a big role in British life, and I often ate lunch in a pub. The restaurant scene in London in 1960 was not exactly famous, but it gradually grew to become internationally renowned. I bought a brand-new Ford and learned to drive on the left. I don't recall making tours, and instead, I used the car to go to the office, where I had a parking space in the office-parking garage. The employees at Bunzl Paper were all much older than I was, so I didn't make friends at the office except with a Viennese executive named Friedl J. David. He was the most productive operator at Bunzl Paper and thus one of the directors. I kept in touch with him during all those years.

It took me a long time to connect with a girlfriend. I finally went to a local dance hall where I met a Spanish girl from Barcelona. We clicked and stayed together for quite a while. I even considered getting engaged with her, but I think my mother discouraged it. Then I met a whole lot of Jewish girls in Hampstead, but it didn't result in a girlfriend. Pattie, as she was known, was a very good-looking and sporty girl, and she was very taken with me, as was I with her. I proposed in time before she and her friend went back to Sydney via a passenger ship, and I talked to her while she was steaming through the Suez Canal. The good thing about working in the UK was that I got four weeks of paid holidays. In 1961, I learned about the French Club Med, and I signed up to spend three weeks at the singles club at Cefalu in Sicily, smack on the Mediterranean Sea. I had to fly to Paris and then rendezvous at a certain bus stop, and from there, we were bused to the train station from where we would board a train to Naples. From Naples, we took a ferry to Palermo and then a bus ride to the Club Med location. The train ride from Paris to Naples was quite a long ride in those days, plus the ferry and finally getting to Club Med. The sleeping arrangements at the club were that three girls occupied one so-called hut and three men another. Shower arrangements were perfect for female and male units.

I was enchanted with all the facilities—the dining hall where we always had a fantastic buffet of tasty dishes three times a day. For dinner, the rose wine was available nonstop in terra cotta jugs. For no reason, I was assigned a hut to myself, so that was convenient all around. I don't recall that we made sightseeing trips into Sicily. Very likely the weather and the beach were so attractive that we stayed around in the club for the whole three weeks. There were not many British girls at the club, and the one we all cherished wasn't going to be a girlfriend to any chap. But we were all good companions. On the way back to Paris, we had time to rummage through Palermo, which I remember with much pleasure, not least because I discovered Dolcelatte cheese, which I shared with my Club Med friends on board the homebound train.

Before completing my two-year stint in London in 1962, I was persuaded by Club Med to be a guest at the opening of their newest club for singles at Acre, Israel. I was offered a four-week stay at the price of three weeks, so I took the bargain.

I had to again fly to Paris and to rendezvous at a bus stop from where a bus ferried us to Charles de Gaulle airport for the flight to Tel Aviv. From Tel Aviv, we bused to Acre. And the arrangements in Acre were quite similar to the Club at Cefalu. The club was not very full despite the gratis fourth week, but within a few days, I got to know a Belgian girl who spoke fluent English, so we got together. As usual, the activities along the Mediterranean make for all sorts of sports on the beach, so we certainly were not bored.

The first time I walked around Acre, it occurred to me that I was on historic grounds in the sense that after 2,000 or so years, Jews had again achieved a Jewish state. I also reminded myself that it had been seventeen years since we were liberated by two Russian soldiers near Tröbitz. At that time, there was a lot of talk about immigrating to Israel, but my mother was adamant that we would immigrate to the United States because her brother was there already. I didn't really know whether the people that I saw on the streets of Acre were Jewish or Arabs, but it didn't matter to me. What mattered was that a Jewish state had arisen from the dust of WWII. I also arranged to see my mother's aunt Lisbet Neu, who had managed to get us the British visas to Palestine. Those legit visas made us "exchange Jews." The idea was that German nationals stuck in Allied countries and who wished to be repatriated to Germany would be exchanged with us. We never got exchanged, but those visas might have saved us from being sent to Auschwitz.

For the fourth week, we had the option to tour Israel and spend a couple of days at a mini Club Med at Eilat on the Red Sea. I don't remember all that we got to see, but we spent one night in Beersheba, so the camel market was a first kind of market for my mates and me. The stay at Eilat was especially unique since it was more like a village than a town at that time. This tour took place fourteen years after the partition, so Israel was still in the process of establishing itself. My second visit to Israel with my sister Erica was in 2016. It was fifty-six years after my Acre Club Med visit to Israel. Obviously, the difference between Israel in 1960 vs. 2016 was enormous and admirable.

My Belgian girlfriend and I traveled back to Paris together, and since she had a friend in Paris who was on holiday elsewhere, we could use her flat for a few days in Paris. That was a very good bonus! All good things come to an end, and we parted company, I returned to London, and she traveled home to Brussels, where she ran a contemporary art store. I once visited her in Brussels when she was home alone, and I enjoyed a nice weekend with her in her parents' bedroom. She took me to the Waterloo battle site, and I am glad I had that historical experience. We also walked through the woods of that area and rested on the moss, and enjoyed the quiet environment.

10

NEW MARRIAGE

I quit Bunzl around April 1962, not because of my salary but because I was homesick to be back in Manhattan, but because Patti would arrive with her parents in the summer to celebrate our wedding in the garden of my mother and Jenö's house in Great Neck, New York.

When I mentioned to Mr. Seton that I wanted to go back to NYC, he had a really good opportunity waiting for me. At that time, a division of Bunzl named Cigarette Components Ltd. had developed a crepe-paper-based cigarette filter. Soon after launching the crepe filter, a more efficient raw material was fabricated from cellulose acetate and was far more efficient for cigarette filter production than crepe. For the filters to be attached to the cigarettes, Hauni, the German cigarette machinery manufacturer, modified the cigarette makers to enable the filters to be automatically attached to the cigarettes, and a whole new so-called healthier filter cigarette came to the market. At its peak rate, Hauni's makers produced 20,000 filter cigarettes/minute. No kidding.

Rudy Bunzl had a 50 percent interest in American Filtrona Corp., dealing with domestic cigarette filter sales, while the other 50 percent was owned by CC Ltd. in London.

American Filtrona, together with CC Ltd., had jointly established Filtrona International Corp. in NYC with John Newman as president (Newman was a friend of Hugo Bunzl from their time in Vienna) for the purpose of managing the export sale of filters throughout the Far East markets. John Newman was about to retire, and I was to take his place. So, departing London was a timely moment as for the next sixteen years, I would run Filtrona International Co. (FIC) from a tiny office at 44th St and Lexington Avenue as the export arm of American Filtrona Inc. located in Richmond, Virginia.

When the wedding with Patti was over, I drove in my new Pontiac convertible via Miami, Florida, where we honeymooned in Richmond. There, I would learn all about filter manufacturing while Patti was at our very comfortable motel. At times I would drive back to the motel to lunch with her. This was a poor beginning for Patti as she was stuck in that room while I absorbed filter making and quality control and even learned the names of the various American cigarette brands and the names of the companies that produced these different brands of cigarettes on the American market and worldwide.

I smoked, but I don't recall which brand. I ceased smoking at age forty.

When my factory training ended, I worked side by side with John Newman and got to know what he had accomplished. It was not much because, for example, he used an agent in Baltimore (which cost us 3 percent commission), whereas I went to visit and sell our filters directly to CAT (Compania Anonima Tabacalera) located in Santiago de los Caballeros, the second largest city after Santo Domingo on in the Dominican Republic. While I was there, I would also fly to Port-au-Prince, Haiti, where there was a small cigarette factory owned by an American who resided in Louisiana. In the future, I would get all the orders directly from LA, and I had a very nice relationship with this owner who kept inviting me to his estate on a Caribbean island, but I never regretfully managed to accept his invitation. Papa Doc was the president of Haiti in those days. I attended a voodoo session just for the sake of knowing what this cult was about. It turned out to be about sacrificing a chicken with a lot of noise. Actually, Port-au-Prince was a lovely city because covered with trees and plants, it smelled rural, chickens and other farm animals walked around town, and there was a very easygoing population. Also, the French cuisine in Port-au-Prince was superb, but it didn't stay that way. A lot of good artists worked in the city, and American tourists, such as my friend Gerry Krefetz and his wife, would buy their paintings and sculptures.

There were three other very small cigarette factories around the Caribbean. One was on Dominica, which was a hard place to fly to, but it was a lovely place to spend a day in this also very green environment. The cigarette factory comprised one cigarette maker behind the counter, and anyone who smoked would buy cigarettes from this shop as fresh as can be. I visited twice, and from then on, the owner sent us his orders in a regular manner. Another similar operator existed on Curacao, and again I visited him once, and then the orders just kept going. The third was a bigger cigarette factory in Belize bordering Guatemala but with the capital Belmopan facing the Caribbean Sea. I visited there twice, and it is a pretty place smack within a big cement seawall one could walk on facing the Caribbean Sea and far more popular nowadays for tourism than it was in the 1960s.

It needs mentioning that it took me a while to understand that adding filters to cigarettes wasn't only a dubious attempt to make smoking less unhealthy but what really made filters popular was that the producers of cigarettes were substituting less costly filters for costlier tobacco— i.e., the filter cigarettes became more profitable. The original filter measured 60mm, but it grew to 120mm in length over time because the profit motive to substitute filters for tobacco was too lucrative to miss.

The year 1978 turned out to be an extremely turbulent year for me. Patti had reached such a degree of anorexia that she had to be rescued via an emergency hospital stay to bring her back to life. It was also the year that Saisampan returned to the United States to earn a second degree in history at NYU that she asked me to write her university application, and she was accepted. It had been about eight years since I was introduced to her at the Greenwich Village dinner with her mother, and during those years, I would have visited at least eight times and at least had one meal with her on each trip. Meanwhile, her mother had given her the business responsibility of Filthai, the local joint venture filter manufacturing operation I had initiated on behalf of CC Ltd in London. Saisampan acquired about one-third of the shares that P. Prachume had invested in Filthai while still earning commissions on sales of filters from Filthai. I also corresponded with Saisampan regularly, and I acted as her New York shopper for whatever needs she had. I don't remember whether she reimbursed me for the shopping I did. When she arrived from Thailand, I had arranged for her to be lodged in a hotel on Madison Avenue, very near to my flat with Patti. I did see her at the hotel, and we sometimes played tennis at a local court. At the end of such a tennis game, Saisampan invited me to her hotel room. That was the moment for her to get close to me.

What followed next was her demand that I divorce Patti. Considering that I had pursued Saisampan via airmail for eight years, there was no alternative but to act accordingly. The time had come to divorce Patti, and Patti went to recover at a psychology clinic outside of

Manhattan at my cost, and I visited her from time to time. Simultaneously I got engaged to Saisampan, and with the help of my mother, we shopped for a diamond ring at the Fifth Avenue diamond stores. After a bit of haggling, we bought a nice diamond ring in a cushioned box for Saisampan, and thereby I figured that we confirmed our engagement, although I had never asked her to marry me.

By then, Saisampan had bought a very nice three-bedroom co-op apartment at the Campanile at 450 East 52nd Street, which is directly across from the prestigious River House. Saisampan often came to lunch with me because we had a mutual taste for an Italian restaurant at the Pan Am Building, which was a short walking distance from my office. During all this upheaval, I suffered from depression. Saisampan blamed it on me regretting the divorce, but after sixteen years of a very unremarkable marriage with Patti without children, there was nothing depressive about making an end with Patti.

Saisampan selected a Japanese psychiatrist who did his best to keep our engagement alive. At that stage of our relationship, Saisampan took the view that I was a "mean old thing," so she referred to me as MOT as my nickname. MOT sounds awful, so I put SA at the end of it to make it sound a bit better—MOTSA. SA is the equivalent in Spanish for Ltd. Did Ltd. send me an internal signal that things were not going as well between us as I had imagined? Perhaps because I am seventeen years older than Saisampan, the "old thing" in MOTSA was her way of putting me off?

Nowadays, Pimoo (Saisampan's Thai nickname) is more likely to call me Papa because that's what Benno called me when he was a little boy. In forty-three years of our marriage, she never addressed me as Ernest or Ernie. Why not? I don't know. Everyone I know had no problem calling me Ernie or Ernest. I even have a friend for the past seventy-four years who insists on calling me Ernesto. Okay! I am making this point not because I demand to be called Ernest or Ernie. MOTSA continued to be more or less my name, except that Papa came up quite often, too. What's in a name? I continue to interpret this question to mean that I, and especially Pimoo, can't escape year after year the fact that I continue to be seventeen years older, and that is irksome for her.

Saisampan liked my beach house at Harvey Cedars on Long Beach Island, and we would drive there often for the weekend. That we had a huge deck on the rear of the house overlooking the bay was due to Patti, who knew from her Australian beach house experiences that a deck is a must, as is an outdoor shower. When you come across the causeway onto Long Beach Island, there is a large fish market in the center of that interchange. We always stopped there and bought giant sea bass (mostly caught by fishermen off the beach at Long Beach Island) that Pimoo cooked very well, and it was a splendid weekend meal. I still had my Pontiac convertible car as well as Kimchee, our pug dog.

Jenö, in particular, was very positively inclined about me marrying Saisampan, and so was my mother. We visited

John Newman in Great Neck, and Mrs. Newman was also very taken with Saisampan.

Saisampan graduated from NYU just in time for me to be required to close the New York office and move back to London. Saisampan was positive about the idea of residing in London. I bought, with the help of a local mortgage, a Mews House in Clabon Mews near Cadogan Square. It turned out we were neighbors of Willy and Mrs. Whitelaw. Willy was the deputy prime minister to Margaret Thatcher. He was an excellent orator, and whenever we happened to see each other as neighbors, he spoke very spontaneously with me. Some years later, he arranged for me to have a permanent UK residence visa, and that visa is still alive. When her husband was named Viscount Whitelaw in 1983, she became Viscountess Whitelaw. However, the lack of a male heir ended the viscountcy with Willy Whitelaw's death. Viscountess Whitelaw subsequently organized a medical device charity for the benefit of the Westminster Hospital, and for many years we were invited to this annual dinner, and we subscribed to her charity.

We got friendly with the builders who had renovated 36 Clabon Mews for a young British couple whose marriage was canceled at the last minute, and hence we happened to buy that house. Arnold Lee was the boss of this group of builders, and he was going to be important for us in due course.

Saisampan didn't like the house much because the rear was devoid of windows, so daylight only reached us from the front of the building. A Mews house such as ours used to be a stable for the residents of Cadogan Square, whose apartment also had no rear windows because the stable and the apartment were equally bricked up.

Nevertheless, we stayed at Clabon Mews for a couple of years because it was spacy and because its garage was big enough for my 250C Mercedes, which I had brought from NYC to London. I quite liked driving on the left in a UK right-side driver's position because I could hug the left side curb closer than British cars driven on the right side could ever hug.

My new London job in 1978 was still related to cigarette filters, but instead of looking after customers, I was now a director of Cigarette Components Ltd., with the responsibility to support the managers of our filter factories in France, Spain, and Brazil. Before I started to exercise that job, Saisampan and I got married at Chelsea Town Hall on November 9, 1978. Her mother, Mrs. Prachume, attended the wedding but morosely. My parents were also witnesses, and they were upbeat about the marriage. We had a catered wedding reception at our Mews house, and it was a very nice party with a lot of my Bunzl colleagues attending, including Mr. G. G. Bunzl.

For our honeymoon, I got permission from Bunzl to fly Concorde, and I paid for Saisampan's ticket, enabling us to fly from London to Acapulco, Mexico, via Paris and Washington, DC. We flew from London to Paris in a commercial plane to board the French Concorde from Charles de Gaulle airport. The first stop was

Washington, DC, and then onwards on the same Concorde to Mexico City. From there, we flew to Acapulco on a domestic Mexican flight.

The Acapulco hotel we stayed at was dedicated to honeymooners. We all had a dipping pool at each house and were delivered a sumptuous breakfast each morning. We enjoyed Acapulco and especially the high skydivers. We also rode on donkeys and enjoyed spicy Mexican food. On the way back, we spent a few days in Mexico City, which was also a new experience for me. It is quite an impressive city with a lot of mural paintings, and the mariachi musical street bands are unique and pleasurable. Mexico City had German restaurants, which were excellent, and we even did a bit of shopping as well. The flight back was via normal commercial planes; I don't recall the route. I was very comfortably seated in the Concorde, but Saisampan didn't like the noise or the little seats. We never did a repeat! Without guzzling champagne, which I did, you might not like Concorde for its noise and small seats.

Since each factory had a manager, I didn't have much to do when I visited these sites. The French factory was a very small operation and managed by an Orthodox Jew, which was quite unusual, but he was seemingly an old friend of Hugo Bunzl, and he liked employing people he considered as family, so that was that. The Spanish factory was located in Guadalajara and was a huge operation in the suburbs of Madrid. So, it meant staying in a Madrid hotel and taxiing to the plant. Madrid is pretty huge so seeing a lot of it wasn't doable.

The Spanish manager was Mariano De Torres R., and so I had a chance to speak Spanish when I met him. For some odd but very nice reason, we used to eat lunch outdoors at the local petrol station, which had a very good café, including choices of wine and those luncheons were remarkable. Since I was excluded from Brazil during my Bogota years, I was keen to be a tourist in Rio de Janeiro for the whole weekend before flying to Sao Paulo to see the Filtrona plant, managed by a very pleasant and capable Italian who married a Brazilian wife, a renowned artist. In Sao Paulo, the factory offered a canteen to the workers, so for lunch, Saisampan and I ate some very good Portuguese meals with the manager. Best of all was the Swiss Hotel in Rio de Janeiro, and not only were the rooms overlooking Copacabana and thus the Atlantic, but the restaurant was superb. Watching the people on the beach playing volleyball was also a good pastime.

None of these managers had any complaints that I could convey to London. Neither could I offer any service to make the plant more profitable. In short, I didn't like that assignment. My expertise was managing sales, and since I was only a few days at each plant, there was no need for me to see the local customers. After several years of handling this job, I was eager to apply for the job of general manager of Cigarette Components Ltd. in London, but it was assigned to a Mr. Williamson, a CC Ltd. scientific researcher who, in my opinion, had no commercial background at all. Hence, in 1980, I resigned pensionless due to having worked both in New York and London for Bunzl, but there was no pension to cover both locations. After twenty years of serving Bunzl, I retired at age forty-eight and somehow missed collecting a pension from either side of the Atlantic except in due course from Uncle Sam at age sixty-five. Much later, Bunzl PLC reversed what had happened with my pension with a minimal pension for life of $378 a month.

On an unexpected occasion, Arnold visited our Mews house, and we told him that I had resigned and planned to go back to NYC. He urged us to stay in London because, at that time, the property development business in London was taking off, and Arnold and the team wanted to benefit from it but needed a source of capital. So, he suggested that we use our capital to acquire dilapidated properties, and he and the team would refurbish and sell them for us.

Saisampan was very much in favor of this project, and not least for reasons that we would have time to enjoy Europe as each project we bought would take about a year to get refurbished and to market. Then we would be in London and cash in and buy a new property with the help of our Natwest Bank. As collateral, we had our residency at 237 Knightsbridge. The second dilapidated property we bought was 237 Knightsbridge, which we bought for a small sum with its sixty-year lease, and after fourteen months of refurbishment, we didn't sell it but instead, we made it our London residence from 1981 until 2008 (twenty-seven years). We sold 237 Knightsbridge in 2007, inclusive of the Freehold (the right to own the land on which 237 stood), and completed the sale in 2008 just before the Great Recession hit the world economy.

Ernest and Saisampan wedding photo at Chelsea Town Hall, London.

Ernest's beloved Mercedes shortly before selling it in 2018

11

CLUB MEDS

My retirement in 1980 provided the opportunity I had been waiting for to spend a whole summer on the Cote d'Azur à la F. Scott Fitzgerald, the author of *The Great Gatsby,* and that is what Saisampan and I did. Except at that time, it didn't occur to me to write a book! We rented a very nice flat in Jean Les Pins, and the facility had an excellent garage, so my car also had a good home. Saisampan was pregnant but still enjoyed the beach, provided there was plenty of shade.

On the second day of our stay, Pimoo (her Thai nickname, which means "small pig") went shopping for two pork chops and walked into the kosher butcher shop on our street. That was a rather bad mistake, but the butchers just had a good laugh and sent her around the corner, where plenty of pork chops were for sale! We had a Boulangerie on our street, so getting fresh baguettes for breakfast every morning was an easy chore.

We used the car a lot to explore places from Nice to Saint-Tropez. Driving on the Grand Cornice is fantastic. The road often runs 500 meters above the sea, offering spectacular views over the Mediterranean coast. An even more delectable destination was San Remo in Italy, not very far and worthwhile for superb luncheons in old-fashioned, high-class Italian restaurants. For example, the waiter would peel a peach in one easy go and serve it as mouth bites on a plate. We loved San Remo also for shopping, and so we got to be frequent visitors. We even spent a few days at a local hotel in San Remo, and that, too, was a delight.

In October, we drove back to London from Jean Les Pins, and 237 Knightsbridge was ready for our occupancy. On January 18, 1981, Benno was born. Why was he called Benno—a German name? Because Saisampan was so certain that she was having a baby girl and was only prepared with girl names. Saisampan was desperate because, based on her Thai family tradition, the name of her offspring must start with a B! Thus, that's how I offered her a boy's name starting with B, and that's how Benno got his first name. I didn't like the German, but my mother's father, Benno Gumperz, would have. Saisampan created a Thai middle name for him as "Baramee," which means "the chosen one." Benno is a very popular Bavarian name because Benno is the patron saint of Munich, where his relics were enshrined in 1580. Saisampan's mother insisted that we get a nanny for Benno, and somehow we got to know Elsie Aurelio, a Filipina who indeed became Benno's nanny but stayed with us until 2008 and gradually became more than a nanny, but a housekeeper, for the four of us. Even up to today, Elsie still comes to Benno's house one day a week to do the cleaning and laundry.

Next door to our 237 was 239 Knightsbridge, which was a baby-care facility. So, we could hand Benno over a low brick wall to one of the caretakers, and he, together with three other babies, were seated in their carriage of four for a daily ride in Hyde Park across the street from us. When Benno got older, Elsie took him to a Montessori school a few blocks down Knightsbridge. So, that was still very convenient for us.

Harrods, the famous and huge department store, is known for being in Knightsbridge, so most tourists go to Knightsbridge, the street we lived on, instead of Harrods on Brompton Road in the district of Knightsbridge. Harrods was our emergency food store if and when we didn't get what we needed from Tesco. To shop at Tesco, one needed a car, so that was my chore.

When Benno was old enough to go to primary school, he got enrolled at a boys'-only school at Eaton House prep school—not a long walk up and down Sloane Street.

Since holidays are quite generous in the UK, we took Benno and Elsie to St. Moritz for Christmas and New Year's and stayed for six weeks as guests in a rental house owned by Mrs. Andreotti. It was a natural opportunity for me to ski. Saisampan didn't ski, but she liked to walk up Corviglia in time for lunch or, if too late to walk, took the funicular train from St. Moritz to the top of Corviglia. We used to eat lunch up there at Mr. Mathis's La Marmite restaurant, which was quite extraordinary as he imported every sort of fresh food and fruit from all over the world. His vast dessert menu was on a table at the entrance to the restaurant and was an immediate attraction once the guests entered. He even had a caviar menu, which was unique. A local St. Moritz entrepreneur, Mr. Glattfelder, hauled caviar using his own plane from Tehran to St. Moritz, which he retailed at a lowish price at his own caviar boutique on Via Maistra, where we often went for an aperitif for me only with a small glass of ice-cold vodka because Pimoo can't digest alcohol, but she and I could enjoy a nice portion of Sevruga caviar before dinner at the hotel. He also provided Mathis's restaurant with all the grades of Iranian caviar that he sold based on his caviar menu!

During one of my earliest experiences at Mathis, I was waiting for Saisampan, and our Swiss waitress asked me where she was from. I told her she was from Thailand. "Well," she said, "you somehow landed someone different, didn't you?" We never forgot that remark and were not sure what she really meant, but Thailand was worth "something different," all right. We didn't mind her remark because, for all we knew, she never had left St. Moritz.

What made the Marmite restaurant even more pleasurable was that the tables were large enough to seat eight guests for lunch, so we always met new people, which was good fun. We reserved space for ourselves often and way ahead with Mrs. Mathis and/or her daughter, who acted as the maître d' at the Marmite restaurant.

St. Moritz village has a twin called St. Moritz-Bad, which is a health spa built over the curative power of the ferruginous and carbonated spring water, which the Romans already used in 1535. We enjoyed taking these mineral baths, as it was very healing, with or without a day of hard skiing.

We often met friends from my Swiss school at St. Moritz. Horea and Vrenni Steiger were often there and Ingrid and Pete Gafgen also. We would have nice company if and when we had drinks at the Polo bar in the Palace Hotel.

Getting to St. Moritz from London took a flight to Kloten, the airport in Zurich. Then there was a passenger train ride from the airport to Chur, and from there onwards, one had to switch to a special mountain train known as the Rhaetian Railway, a train through many tunnels and bridges and nonstop mountains on either side and at the end of the line was St. Moritz. I always enjoyed the views from that train and more so lunching in the dining car and, being Swiss, the choice of dishes on that train was quite surprisingly good. I liked eating on that moving train through all that wintery scenery. It was truly exciting, but Saisampan didn't much like the three-hour train ride, although once in St. Moritz, with its super luxury shops and its attractive footpaths from one village to another village, she liked that. The Cresta Tobogganing Club is also a famous sport in St. Moritz, but I never went on the Cresta ice run. Horse racing on Lake St. Moritz is another winter sport, and people can be seated on temporary stands on the frozen lake to watch the race and even bet on a horse.

St. Moritz became for us the standard winter holiday, usually after Christmas and New Year, which was the highlight of the season that we skipped. Instead, we started going to Fort Lauderdale in Florida during Christmas and New Year's, where we had been recommended an apartment hotel, which is far more convenient than a hotel. We would fly from London to Miami and then taxi to Ft. Lauderdale. The hotel had a huge swimming pool within their generous garden, and the beach was just a few more meters further. We liked being in Ft. Lauderdale with Benno and Elsie.

While Benno was still young, we would take him to NYC to stay at Saisampan's flat in the Campanile Co-Op, and we enjoyed spending holiday time in Manhattan. The superintendent remembered us and invited us to see the empty three-floor apartment that belonged to the Heinz food family. The middle floor was, no kidding, a ballroom. The kitchen and dining rooms were on another floor and outfitted extra voluptuously with a variety of oyster dishes. We didn't see the bedrooms. Those three floors ended up being refurbished into three separate apartments. The Heinz flat goes back to the golden age of the roaring twenties. Greta Garbo also had a whole floor at the Campanile Co-Op, which she occupied singly until she died at age eighty-five in 1990, and the apartment was sold for $9 million because it contained all her belongings.

We wheeled Benno through the area of our Manhattan residence, and he always was too hot or at least didn't like to wear socks and managed to slide them off, and other walkers would bring them back to us! Elsie was with us taking care of Benno, and we would dine out often and enjoy the New York restaurant scene again.

This was also the beginning of going to family Club Meds (vs. singles-only clubs) with a children's club (run by GOs = Gentil Organisateurs), and these staff members were very well trained and most helpful in keeping all children busy and supervised from 9 a.m. to 6 p.m. So, at 6 p.m., he would get a quick bath and be ready with other children to watch the daily GOs' show, often with professional acrobats or otherwise talented GOs. In other words, Club Med made sure that the children were kept busy so that the parents could benefit from the sports facilities the club offered.

Our first such club was in a suburb of Athens, Greece, and our London friends Anna and Peter Clarke, with two small girls, enticed us to join them at this family Club Med in Greece. Subsequently, we went to Club Meds in the Caribbean—i.e., St. Lucia, Dominican Republic, and Eleutheria in the Bahamas. We also enjoyed the club on Corsica, although the drive from the airport to the club was so winding that almost everyone on the bus got carsick. That was not a problem at Club Med in Marbella, Spain, which was super deluxe. The pink sand of Eleutheria was spectacularly fine, and we went there twice as well as two times to St. Lucia. We also went to North Africa, where a great family Club Med was located in Tunisia. After Tunisia, we joined a family Club Med in Turkey with Benno and spent two weeks there. I don't know in which month we went, but it was mighty hot and impossible to walk barefoot on the sand.

The routine of Club Med was always the same, which made going to different clubs very easy. Saisampan and I joined a club excursion to see a whole range of Roman ruins. The Turkish/French cuisine was very satisfying, as was the wine. Then, one day, Club Med offered a five-masted computer-controlled staysail schooner operated as a cruise ship. Peter Clarke and family alerted us again to this cruise, and we joined them. Corfu was the place from which we had to board the Club Med schooner. We arrived a few days earlier to play tourist on Corfu. While there, we stayed at a Hilton hotel, which was built too near to the airport because each time a plane took off, it sounded like it flew through our bedroom. Nevertheless, we enjoyed the hotel, the sightseeing on Corfu, and on the walk down to the beach, there was a Greek food vendor doing barbecued fish on his cart. We liked what he cooked! We had a cabin for three on that schooner, which was just perfect with Benno onboard with us. I don't remember all the ports we visited, but Capri was one we enjoyed a lot. The final destination of the cruise was Cannes in France.

．　．　．

When Saisampan got bored in London and wanted to go back to university, I suggested that she get a law degree, and so she was admitted to SOAS (School of Asian Studies). She also took a course in Buddhism. That was the start of her devotion to Buddhism and meditation. The university had a seven-day "reading holiday," enough for us to spend time on islands in the Caribbean without Club Meds, but just on our own. Our first trip to St. Barth for the seven days of reading was a huge success, and we repeated this routine in due course. We flew from London to Antigua, from where we were fetched by Captain Remy de Haenen, the original owner of the Eden Rock Hotel in St. Bartholomew, in his four-seater Cessna plane. He flew us to St. Barth. Remy was the first pilot to ever land on St. Barth. His Eden Rock facility was superbly located, and we often had lunch there. Remy suggested that he fly us to neighboring islands such as Saba, Montserrat, and Saint Kitts and Nevis. That way, we visited these neighboring islands, and he got a nice lunch with us and never charged us for the short-distance flights. He would buy local food items in some of those islands and then fly us back to St. Barth.

On another occasion, we spent the seven days on St. Maarten, a Dutch possession. Barbados also got us enchanted, not least for the flying fish, which were very tasty. We can't omit that we also liked to holiday on Aruba as well as on Martinique and finally, we also discovered Grenada, all without Club Meds! So, with or without Benno, we certainly got to enjoy the pleasures of these Caribbean Islands.

I don't want to belittle Kingston, Jamaica, because, in the 1950s, I visited there several times. I stayed at the Blue Mountain Hotel, where I was introduced to Sir Alexander Bustamante, the prime minister of Jamaica. I can only imagine that this introduction occurred due to my surname! Years later, when I flew on Lufthansa from JFK to Lima, Lufthansa made a stopover in Kingston, Jamaica. I got off the flight because I had organized my itinerary to spend the weekend at Morgan Harbor, Jamaica, and then pick up Lufthansa again on Monday onwards to Lima. I had paper and board customers in Kingston. On other occasions, when I flew from JFK to Kingston, I would continue the flight to Montego Bay for the weekend. My agent had recommended a boarding house in Montego Bay, and I loved the beach.

That evening I went at a dusky time for a walk on the beach, and I encountered a Jamaican girl. I even remember that she wore an orange dress. I am not sure whether my agent arranged for her to pleasure me, but whether he did or not, we had a go on the soft beach all by ourselves. Just to not get a bad idea, no money changed hands. In Jamaica, I came across a high-alcohol white-colored rum, which was too potent for my taste. It was used by the sugar cane cutters to keep the tough job going!

When Benno was ready for university, he opted for Edinburgh University—naturally, as far as possible from home! He also figured that choosing to read History of Art was the easiest curriculum to take for four years. It turned out to be mighty difficult. Nevertheless, he carried on reading and learning, and meanwhile, we went and explored new locations to enjoy.

Sardinia, which is an Italian Island in the Mediterranean Sea, is a gem. The Cala di Volpe was the most famous hotel in the world. We were there when the Aga Khan was still the owner. Nowadays, Starwood manages the hotels under a long-term contract and retains a 49 percent stake in the undeveloped land. The restaurant at Cala di Volpe was, and probably still is, the most elegant restaurant and most delicious restaurant in the world as well. From Porto Cervo to Venice, one is still in Italy, and the luxury at the Cipriani is on a different level but still very enchanting because Venice doesn't have all that space that Sardinia offers.

If nothing else, the Cipriani is the only Venice hotel with an outdoor Olympic-size swimming pool. The rooms are splendidly antique. The Terrace restaurant is the highlight of one's stay at the Cipriani, and we went there more than once. The flight from London to Venice is quite easy, and there is a slew of motorboats in the nearby harbor to whisk one to whichever hotel one is booked.

Getting lost while walking in Venice is standard fare and is what makes discovering Venice so nice. We used to telephone Jenö from Piazza San Marco because he was a great fan of Venice, and he took great pleasure in knowing that we were there. Another culinary aspect of

Venice is Mr. Harry Cipriani, who no longer owns the hotel and runs Harry's Bar & Restaurant not far from where the Cipriani Hotel shuttle boat lands. Not only is the food at Harry's good everyday Italian food, but the clientele is especially worthy of observing at both the bar and in the downstairs restaurant. We made many table bookings at Harry's and had our own best table and "our" own waiter! But even more interesting, I had a chance to chat with Harry. On such an occasion, I told Harry that a certain dessert I had eaten at the Cipriani restaurant in Monte Carlo was better than the one in Venice! This excited Harry, and he told his chef to match the recipe for that cake with the Monte Carlo's recipe so that I could judge whether it was now as good as in Monte Carlo.

Every evening I was given a huge piece of cake to test. I didn't want to hog it, so I passed it on to nearby guests who liked the idea of getting involved in this tasting event. After three goes, Harry won the test because I judged that the Venice cake was now as good as the Monte Carlo cake! I think that Harry had assumed that I was a member of the Hilton chain, and therefore he wanted/needed to please me.

We discovered that Palma de Mallorca was still quite warm in October. So, since we liked being in Palma, we managed to rent a fabulous flat overlooking the garden, pool, and the sea. The balcony of our two-bed apartment was almost bigger than the apartment itself. So that was our September residence in Palma de Mallorca. Saisampan preferred to swim in the sea, while I preferred doing laps in the pool. In October, we "moved" away from the sea to Avenida, Argentina, where we also rented a two-bedroom apartment in an Art Deco building. What made it a special location was that a short walk behind the condo was the Mercado Santa Katarina, which is a delightful, covered food market but also a chance to buy fresh fish and pass it over to a bar where it would be cooked as per one's wish. We visited Santa Katarina Market almost daily while on Avenida Argentina in Palma de Mallorca.

On one occasion, we invited Benno, now married to Vicki Clements, to spend time with us at our September Palma site, and we managed to get them a modern flat within walking distance from ours. The next time we got them into a nice hotel also within walking distance of our rental.

While my mother and Jenö were alive, I would visit them occasionally while residing at the Greenhill Apartments in Wynnewood, Pennsylvania, where my sister Erica had a penthouse. Once I was in Philadelphia, then I would spend a few days in Manhattan at the Lombardy Apartment Hotel, which I had frequented for years due to Graham Rogoff's recommendation. I still had Gerry Krefetz, a Columbia University friend whom I could visit, and that was one good reason to be in NYC. I also used the opportunity to buy the latest ASICS shoes, which had become the daily shoe for me due to their gel and great rubber heel. For Jenö's 100th birthday, Gerry joined me to celebrate his centenary.

Saisampan graduated from SOAS, but now she had to decide whether to become a solicitor at a firm of solicitors or to become a barrister. In the UK, the solicitor is equivalent to a US lawyer, whereas a barrister is a lawyer who gets selected by a solicitor to take a case to court. In other words, court cases are always dependent on a barrister who is focused on a particular aspect of the law, whereas Saisampan specialized in family law. To be a barrister, you become a member of a chamber where all barristers are practicing family law, for example. Saisampan had to travel around the UK to appear in court cases. So, this was a demanding job—not least of which was the train ride. Unfortunately, she had to quit this profession because she lost her hearing, and even with hearing aids, it was too risky to go to court and risk not hearing precisely what was being said.

She did handle cases in Thailand because she could write her opinions and so was still able to practice.

While Arnold was refurbishing, and we were selling refurbished apartment buildings, the business was reaching a crescendo, and we managed to sell our final and largest project ever to the Chinese Oil Company for their staff in London. It was just in time because, in 2008, the Great Recession took place, and the London property development business collapsed. But we had sold before the collapse!

The same goes for 237 Knightsbridge, which we also sold in 2007 because, after twenty-six years of residing at 237 Knightsbridge SW7 1DJ, Benno was now twenty-six years old and wanted a bachelor's flat. We bought him a raised first-floor dilapidated one-bedroom flat at Ladbroke Square, but Arnold wasn't able to do the refurbishing job, so the architect who handled the refurbishment had a team of Polish builders who did a good job too.

Our purchase and final sale before the Great Recession in 2008 was just in time—except that we were unable to find a suitable new residence for ourselves. We finally settled on a six-month rental on Eton Square.

While that rental was so-so, we still liked living on Eton Square. Consequently, when a two-bed flat was available on the second floor at 58 Eton Square, we bought the ten-year available lease. Our address was within easy walking distance to Sloane Square, where a tube station was located. Actually, we had two tube stations within easy walking, as Victoria Station wasn't far away either. Eton Square is about as posh as anything in Belgravia. Looking north, we could see the other side of Eton Square, which was considered even posher in the sense that the flats were generally bigger than on the south side. Still, we had a beautiful view since there were nonstop gardens in front of the building as well as private gardens in the rear of the building. It also was easy to find space to park my car on the street because I had a parking permit based on our Eton Square residency.

Ten years later, our Eton Square lease was up. We packed our belongings and had them shipped to BKK. I couldn't import my used car into Thailand, so I sold it to a friend of Benno's. So, in 2018 we were back in our condo rental flat in BKK. A year later, the unexpected pandemic hit the world, and we continued to live healthily in our three-bedroom rental flat on Radjadamri Road and admired the extraordinary way the government managed COVID-19, which during sixteen months killed only ninety-five virus victims out of a population of 70 million. Things didn't work as well in 2021 because many variants of the original virus made the pandemic even more complex.

Ernest skiing in St Moritz in the 1980s.

Ernest and Benno 1985, Pattaya Thailand.

Ernest and Saisampan at her graduation
ceremony from SOAS 1993.

Jenö at his 100th birthday party,
Philadelphia, 22 April 1995.

Ernest and Gerry Krefetz at Jeno's 100
birthday. 22 April 1995.

Erica and Ernest at Benno Hilton and Vicki
Clements wedding. London, 19 May 2015.

12

WORLD TRAVELER

Gradually, I learned a lot from my mentor Tom Greiner at the office of American Paper & Pulp. When I volunteered to be the sales manager on site in South America from 1958 onward, with my headquarters in Bogota, I must have learned a lot without even realizing it. I didn't even realize that I had a salesman's knack as well as a very easy way to socialize with my few new friends in Bogota and elsewhere in South America as well as with our South American agents and customers.

I didn't attend any movies or concerts, but I got invited to Sunday-afternoon bullfights in Bogota and Lima. A bullfight begins with selecting whether to sit in the shade or the sunny side. To watch the picadors, on their trained horses, get the bull angry, and the matador perform his ballet-like maneuvers called for a good sip of wine now and then from the wineskin we carried into the corrida. The matador's colorful outfit, and especially the way he handles his cape, is exciting. It takes a lot of courage as well as great agility to elegantly get out of the way of a charging bull, and most of the time, the matador manages it. If he manages a clean kill with his sword, then the whole arena gets to cheer him on. Removing the bull's carcass from the arena is a sad spectacle, but it provides a lot of good meat. So, the spectacle ending inevitably in death has sadness for some softhearted individuals like me and for those who claim to be aficionados of the corrida who can't wait for the next week's fight.

Somehow, I liked the Lima bullring better than the one in Bogota. In Lima, the ring might have been more luxurious than in Bogota. Also, there were a lot of food vendors when one exited the arena, and this gave us a chance to eat grilled goat meat, which was not only an unusual snack but a very tasty one. This reminds me that in Lima, in the autumn, there is a religious holiday known as "the Feast of the Lord of Miracles," when all the people wear purple clothes and Catholic icons are carried around town. The street vendors are again very active, selling all sorts of chicken offal such as grilled livers and hearts. I liked that too and still do!

Once I resigned from being an employee in 1980 at age forty-eight, Saisampan and I spent a lot of time traveling to a variety of very attractive European destinations. Since Saisampan spent six months at the Sorbonne while a student at Boston University, she was just as keen to be in Paris as I was. In those days, getting a Parisian hotel reservation was quite difficult. They were sold out whenever we wanted to have a room. Jenö recommended

Hotel De La Tremoille Hotel on 4 Rue de la Tremoille because he and my mother stayed at that hotel many times. We did manage to get reservations without using my parents' name, which wouldn't have made any sense. We liked the hotel and more so the location. On one occasion, we had a reservation, but they couldn't honor it and instead gave us the Satchmo suite, which was the most expensive suite in the hotel, but they only charged us what our room would have cost. It was a real eye-opener to get into such a luxury setup, and we enjoyed it a lot, including the presence, for me, of a trouser press, which is very British.

However, Saisampan had the good idea that instead of getting a Paris hotel reservation, we ought to buy ourselves a small flat. Whenever in Paris, we would spend a lot of time in the 6e arrondissement, and therefore we visited the very few estate agents in that area to offer us an apartment in the 6e that we could afford. Most were too costly, but one day we were shown a totally newly refurbished 22-square-meter mini flat on 36 Rue de Buci. I fell in love with the location and the apartment, too, because it had two huge windows looking down on an inner courtyard, which made the place appear a bit larger and definitely quiet and airier. We bought it, and our lawyer and friend of Saisampan, Pierre Cola de la Noue, handled all the paperwork in conjunction with Paul Wurtzel, our lawyer from New Jersey.

The first thing we had to do to the flat was to increase the security of our front door as we were burgled soon after we moved in. In 1981, when we bought the flat on Rue de Buci, the street had oodles of useful shops and, surprisingly, even a horse butcher shop, which we found quite exceptional. We did try a horse meat steak and found it so-so. Nevertheless, we were pleased with our freedom to go to Paris whenever we wished, although it would be a while before the Eurostar existed, and so we either flew to Paris or took the ferry.

The flat had a kind of Pullman kitchen and a decent bathroom with a tub, and the rest of the flat was either a bedroom or a lounge, depending on the time of day! For the bedroom, we had brought our Castro convertible couch from New York to London and now moved it from London to Rue de Buci, where it was just right. The British hauler who handled the Castro convertible was a one-man operation. Since the Castro was mighty heavy, he traveled to Paris with a bottle of whiskey. He then selected a strong-looking chap on Rue de Buci and offered him a bottle of whiskey to help him get the Castro from the van up the stairs to the second floor with him and into our flat. How about that!? Good thinking he had!

When Saisampan wanted to nap, I was told to go to a café downstairs and sit it out while she slept. The apartment had electric heating, so we could even use it in the winter, although I don't remember going in the winter. It is worthwhile to recall that in those days, we had to buy French francs with whatever money we had, and this was always a time-consuming chore—not only to find a bank doing foreign exchange but getting the bank with the most favorable exchange rate. When the Euro currency came on the scene, we were grateful because we could finally travel around Europe without needing a foreign exchange bank. Just thinking about the trouble it caused makes me aware of how lucky we are that the euro currency came alive and spared us the continuous loss of exchange costs.

Among our favorite restaurants in the 6e was/is Brasserie Lipp at 151 Blvd. saint Germain 6e. A less posh but still excellent restaurant choice was a chain of Parisian restaurants named Le Relais de L'Entrecôte, which we often visited even if we had to queue because it was worth it. Not only was the food excellent, but also it was served in two segments. A first go, and when your plate was eaten clean, the waitress would serve you the other half equally warm and tasty. Nobody had trouble eating the second half. Not only that, but the dessert menu was a huge selection of traditional French desserts, and we had no hesitation in indulging.

However, when it came to great French cuisine, we loved being invited to chez Pierre's home for dinner, where his wife, Mireille, would cook a fantastic menu for that evening, and we had great culinary joy from the appetizers to the dessert and lots of wine in between. Pierre's mate from his days in school is Gilles de Toulgoet. Gilles had a partner in the art business and worked in the refurbishment of dilapidated castles in France. We were lucky to be invited to stay at two different castles they had fixed up, and it was a unique event for us to be in that kind of spacious surroundings and décor as well as freshly created outdoor spaces. In due course, they had sold both castles.

Talking about splendid places in France, I took Patti in the 1960s for a vacation at the Residence de la Reserve, a first-class hotel in Beaulieu-sur-Mer. It is an enormously solid old hotel facing the Mediterranean from a huge outdoor luncheon veranda overlooking the fine swimming pool and access to the sea via steps.

The reclining chairs around the pool at La Reserve Hotel were wonderfully comfortable, and I hope they still have those nowadays. The hotel's deluxe store was very attractive too, and I still have a huge beach towel that I bought there.

The rooms are very airy and decent size but also not overly decorated. The dining hall was very impressive in size and heavily decorated, but the cuisine was light and faultless. Even the bar area was big, and the service was first class, even when ordering a martini. I think that Jenö also recommended that hotel to me. Not far from the hotel was a small but very nice sandy beach, so that was good for swimming in the Mediterranean. We also could take the train and ride to Nice and go shopping there. The beach restaurants in Nice are world renowned, as is the Promenade des Anglais. While in Nice, one should also visit the Chagall and the Matisse museums, both of which are extra popular with me!

Years later, Saisampan and I rented Villa Margarita for a month that came with a narrow but long swimming pool way up on a hill overlooking Beaulieu-sur-Mer and the Mediterranean. To get to town, we had to walk a rather steep up or down set of steps down about twenty-five minutes to the center of Beaulieu and a thirty-five-minute walk up to get back to our villa. At that center, there was a weekly market, and we liked buying all sorts of fruits, vegetables and cheeses, and whatever else we needed from the nearby supermarket. We would then have to go to the railway station to queue for a taxi to bring us up the hill and into the courtyard of Villa Margarita.

We invited Pierre and family and Gilles as guests, and they enjoyed a chance to be on the Cote. Saisampan's best Thai girlfriend, Khun Nee, worked as a BKK tourist guide, and it so happened that she took a group of twelve high-social-standing Thais on a cruise, which was to anchor for a few hours in Beaulieu, and she arranged for two big people carriers to ferry this group of friends to our villa for lunch. For such a crowd, we had arranged for a professional chef and waiter, and the lunch was a big success. But, more so, these momentary guests fancied our villa overlooking Beaulieu and the Mediterranean Sea and couldn't say enough good things about our holiday location. It was a rushed drive back to the cruise ship, but they made it.

From Beaulieu, we could go for a nice walk around Cap-Ferrat, which is the most luxurious of all communities on the Cote. On another occasion, we had the pleasure of visiting the Villa Ephrussi, which used to be the summer home of the Rothschilds on the Cote. The gardens of that villa are beyond description, but the whole setup is superb, and we can recommend that day trip to whoever gets to enjoy the Cote. St. Jean is a town before one gets to Cap-Ferrat with an excellent wine shop where I could buy a rare bottle of Clos de Mouches from Joseph Drouhin's estate. Even more worthwhile was to spend a lunch or dinner at La Voile d'Or Hotel, where you can also arrive at its own yacht harbor.

We were aware of Monte Carlo for a very different kind of extreme luxury, but we nevertheless spent now and then at least a week or two at Club Monte Carlo, very near the Monte Carlo tennis club. We had a two-bed flat-like accommodation with an entrance from the hall and from the outside steps. We were able to walk out of the apartment to the Olympic-size swimming pool, which was especially nice early in the morning. However, Saisampan, as usual, preferred to swim in the sea, so she had easy access in and out of the sea directly in front from our outside exit. Breakfast on the veranda was served pleasurably as well as consumed with gusto. Walking around Monte Carlo was not only fun, but it was a safe and secure place. We didn't go to the casino because I had done that on a prior visit, and Saisampan had no interest in gambling. For dinner, we liked the Cipriani restaurant not only for the Italian cuisine but also for the variety of overdressed ladies and their partners. The valet parking was very active, and the variety of up-market cars was worth watching for a while. We had no car, so we walked to and from the restaurant, and that was just as well because we ate heartily. To keep our weight down, we had a French gym trainer two days a week on the grounds of the club, and he was very professional.

Talking about the Cote d'Azur, I once had the pleasure of riding a train pulled by a steam locomotive from Marseille to Nice. I met Mr. Newman in Marseille because he was on holiday in that area. The rendezvous' purpose was to get his agreement for me to go ahead and start a joint venture filter factory in Manila with our Manila agents. We both ate Bouillabaisse in Marseille (Marseille is famous for that dish), and I got his okay to proceed with the joint venture in Manila. We then parted company, and I spent one night in Marseille. The following day, the ride from Marseille to Nice on the track puffing along the Mediterranean coast provided a great hope to one day spend a whole summer on the Cote d'Azur. The conductor pointed out the villa of Somerset Maugham on that ride, and since I had read a lot of his stories and books, I was fully aware of how majestic it must be to have a villa along the Cote.

That night I stayed at the Negresco Hotel, which is one of the most ancient and famous hotels in Nice. The hotel needed a refurbishment in 1962 (which they got but much later), but I never used it again because it was too stodgy and too pricey. The next day I flew from Nice to Manila. I don't remember the route we flew, but from Nice to Manila is 6,644 air miles, so very likely we had to refuel somewhere.

From 1962 onward, my job at Filtrona was not only demanding but also very successful. Globalization wasn't a concept then, but when I suggested a joint venture manufacturing opportunity in Manila, I got the OK, and within less than a year, the Manila plant was producing and selling filters to the Philippine cigarette industry (very big) and instead of shipping from Richmond, Virginia, to markets in the Far East, we now had a Manila base from which we could serve our Far East customers faster and cheaper. Globalization had arrived for me without disrupting the Richmond plant.

While the Manila plant was in the process of being established, I arranged my itinerary to spend the weekend in Honolulu on the way to Manila. I did that several times the first time staying at the Royal Hawaiian Hotel, which is unique and very close to the wide beach area. Surfing is the big sport in Honolulu, and I took several lessons but failed to get the hang of it. On another occasion, I booked a bungalow at the Hilton Waikoloa Village. They were very private, and they turned out to be useful. One evening at the restaurant where I was dining alone, I was invited by a middle-aged British lady to join her on the dance floor. She was holding me very close, and I got the vibes she was sending me. So, when there was a pause, she suggested we go to her room. I suggested she come to my bungalow as it is cozier and nearer to the beach. Since I was booked to depart for Manila early the next morning, I got the concierge to change my departure by one night, which worked. So, she stayed with me until morning, and then she wanted to go to her room and meet me later on the beach with her parents. Indeed, I got to meet her elderly parents, and the four of us walked on the beach for a good while, but there was no discussion about the prior night of lovemaking.

Many years later, I also took Saisampan and Benno to that Hilton Hotel in Hawaii, but the bungalows I had enjoyed were either gone or not suitable for three occupants. Anyhow, we enjoyed staying at this hotel because the beach area was huge and very accommodating. We also drove around the island and saw the environment and, in particular, pineapple plantations. We then decided we wanted to be in Honolulu, and we switched to a Japanese hotel not far from the Royal Hawaiian Hotel. Walking through Honolulu was quite nice, and Benno was keen to eat breakfast at McDonald's, which didn't suit us, but we let him have his way. Neither I nor we ever explored any of the other Hawaiian Islands, but we were satisfied enough with what we had enjoyed on the Big Island.

Many years later, on October 1, 1975, I was the lucky person to be in Manila just in time to attend the "Thrilla in Manila" final boxing match between Muhammad Ali and Joe Frazier. It took place in the Araneta Coliseum in Cubao, Quezon City. My American lawyer Bob Quasha had invited me to join him. Shortly after we found our seats, President Marcos entered the arena with great applause from all the fans, but not from Mr. Quasha. Why? Because Marcos had recently raised the import duty for tow (the raw material for filter manufacturing)—only for Filtrona—so high so as to enable his friend at Zuellig Corp. to be the sole filter manufacturer in the Philippines.

Quasha was so outraged at this unscrupulous presidential decree that effectively wiped Filtrona from the Philippine market that in my presence at his office, he declared that his firm would fight this case against Marcos to the bitter end. This was a nice gesture, but by the time the import duty was again at the original level for everyone, the Filtrona factory had been closed, and its machinery was shipped elsewhere.

It is worthwhile noting that Quasha served on the staff of General MacArthur in the Pacific and reached the rank of lieutenant colonel. He won a Bronze Star and the Philippine Legion of Honor and Liberation Medal. After the war, he stayed in Manila and formed his law firm known as Quasha Ancheta Pena & Nolasco.

Meanwhile, I established joint filter factories in Taiwan, Bangkok, and Medan, Sumatra. So, our capacity was not only for the local demand, but each factory could export to those who needed filters in the Far East.

Once smoking became less and less popular for health reasons, Bunzl spun off the whole worldwide Filtrona filter manufacturing business to a new owner who used the name Essentra.

The Medan, Sumatra, factory that I initiated was moved to Yogyakarta on Java, where it became the most productive filter factory in the world due to demand in nearby China, where 300 million people still smoked filter cigarettes.

Saisampan's mother, Mrs. Prachume, owned six traditional Thai beach houses on some property beyond Pattaya. Saisampan, Benno, Elsie, and I used the best-located beach house in that cluster for our Thai beach holidays. It's about a three-hour drive to that location from BKK. The beach houses stood on four very high pillars, so we were always climbing steps to get to one huge raised room from where we could see the sea. Everybody slept on some side of that room and showered on the ground floor by dipping into a huge vessel with water and tossing the cool water over our heads.

The kitchen and so-called dining room were also on the ground floor, and we had a local cook who cooked for us daily. The location was very rural, and across from our beach house was a home with a rooster that woke me every morning around 5 a.m. I was not amused, but we couldn't silence him! During the day, we would stay on the beach on comfortable beach chairs under palm trees, and vendors would pass and sell local delicacies, and we indulged in everything. I also was invited to learn to sail a boat, and that was a lot of fun, although I didn't get that many lessons. We swam in the sea, and one day, Benno got bitten by a stingray, and he was in great pain. Saisampan knew a monk in the woods behind our beach house, and he had some medication. He blew air on the wound, and Benno recovered after a while. In the evenings, Saisampan and I went to Pattaya town to watch a show of this or that, and we probably ate there as well.

Many years later, when Mrs. Prachume retired from her office work, and she moved to a new location, she arranged for all six beach houses to be disassembled so that they could be re-erected on her new home property. The idea was to rent space to those who needed space. I never visited her in that new location.

That change of events brought a new beach house for consideration by a friend. A Thai girlfriend of Saisampan —then and now residing in Lugano, Switzerland and running a Thai restaurant—named Oy was married to Jacques, who is now sadly deceased. She knew that a developer had built a huge new compound with seventy-one beach houses named Baan Sra Suan in Hua Hin, only about two-and-a-half hours from BKK. The developer had gone bankrupt, and his house was the only one available for sale and was the most well-located semidetached house within the compound. So, we inspected it, and Oy, Saisampan, and I well-liked it a lot. So, the two of them bought it jointly. Since we were In BKK whereas Oy and Jacque were in Lugano, we used it more than they did. Baan Sra Suan has a fantastic swimming pool because it reaches each unit within a few meters from each front door. Each house is three stories high, a total of 210 square meters, with three double bedrooms with showers. In those days, I had an international driver's license and drove from our BKK condo to Hua Hin. When we had possession of the property, Oy and Jacque came, and together we decorated and jointly bought furniture that the house needed.

Whenever we spent time at that beach house, we had a local maid to clean it and do our laundry and, above all, buy fresh seafood from the local market and arrange it for our lunch with or without some friends visiting. After a good number of years of usage, Oy wanted to be bought out, and so Saisampan bought her share, and now the house was totally in her name. Now that it was hers, she made a lot of small and big refurbishments. The actual beach was only a five-minute walk via the rear exit of the compound. When the tide was out, everyone came to walk on the beach or rent a horse.

During that time, an airplane connection came into use so that one could arrive from London at Suvarnabhumi airport and transfer to a nine-passenger plane for the thirty-minute flight to the Hua Hin airport. That was a really fine connection, but it didn't last long because not enough passengers used the air service.

Eating from the extra-long pier over the sea was a big deal for having dinner in Hua Hin town. A Hilton hotel was also built in Hua Hin, and we used to eat there too from the upper level of the high-rise hotel providing great views over the town and sea. Last but not least, there is a night market in Hua Hin where just about everything can be bought, so it attracts most tourists. We used to be good customers of an ice cream vendor because her ice cream was so good that she even served it at the royal palace. So, in addition to our very satisfying condo in BKK near Lumpini Park and opposite the Royal Thai Sports Club, we now had the opportunity to change the environment by going to Baan Sra Suan, where our beach house was awaiting us. Years later and due to the pandemic, we don't dare to mingle with people, so we haven't used it almost for the past two years now.

13

AMERICAN AS APPLE PIE

In 1995, I became an entrepreneur by opening the Montignac Café and Boutique on 160 Old Brompton Road. The whole story about that business revolved around the ongoing desperate topic of dieting.

After twelve years of really hard work in the catering business, I decided to sell the store and handed the sales task to a property sales agent. It so happened that my chef and one of his relatives were keen to acquire my store, so I sold it to them in 2007—yes, once again, in time for me not to be hit by the Great Recession, although I was sorry for my chef who didn't deserve such very bad luck since all businesses suffered badly from then on for a long while. Yes, we were lucky again because the revenue from the shop's sales price happened to be the equivalent, less the sales commission, to the total investment I had made in the business during the twelve years of my catering career.

For the last word, I want to say that I think my autobiography is quite unusual because, despite the Holocaust, I had such a good career and was carefree enough to retire at a young age so that I could also enjoy the pleasure of not working the standard routine until exhausted at age sixty-five, retirement age. When I did tackle entrepreneurship, it turned out to be worthwhile, although the boutique was mostly hard work and no reward except for recovering all the investments I had made in the business.

You appreciate the idea of freedom after you are, year after year, trapped behind barbed wires, plus a tower at every corner with an armed guard. Your oppressors make you fall into a daily count, congregating at 7 a.m. to make sure that no prisoner had somehow escaped. The only escape from a concentration camp to freedom is when you get shot dead attempting to escape. Freedom is only understood and appreciated if one has been incarcerated.

Now that we are in the midst of a roaring pandemic, the word freedom is being tossed around like free lollypops at a party for the sake of avoiding the simplistic protocol to prevent people from catching the virus or, even more, to prevent one from inadvertently infecting your loved ones or your neighbors. If you think wearing a mask or being alert to social distancing is an infringement on your freedom, you are selfishly and very dangerously risking your life, your family's lives, and, yes, your neighbors' lives! Freedom isn't easily acquired in America for about 20 percent of the population that isn't earning enough income to be free from the daily stress to make ends meet.

Freedom, without enough daily funds to make ends meet, is oppression. This issue of extreme inequality is a blight on Americans who toil day and night and are nevertheless short of money for their daily needs, let alone to pay their monthly rent, etc. Everybody knows about this catastrophic condition because it is contrary to our democracy.

President Biden will rectify this grotesque situation via a hike to a $15-per-hour minimum wage, which can fill the current income gap. By filling that gap, freedom from financial distress will be achieved.

I am reaching the end of my biography. I have given you "complete" insight into surviving the Holocaust, my schooling, my character, my career, my wives, and how I managed my leisure time. My career was totally based on one basic raw material—namely cellulose. I have also given you a huge insight into both my business travel as well as a lot of my private travel, always with Saisampan.

I assume that I will spend the rest of my life in Bangkok because of the agreeable tropical climate, its modest cost of living, and its up-to-date health services, which are excellent and reasonably priced.

It needs to be mentioned that every Thai compound, private house, store, and even every huge Condo skyscraper has/must have a "spirit house" in front of it. A spirit house is a shrine to the protective spirit of a place that is found in the Southeast Asian countries of Burma, Cambodia, Laos, Thailand, Malaysia, Indonesia, Vietnam, and the Philippines. The spirit house is normally in the form of a small-roofed structure and is mounted on a pillar or on a dais.

A spirit house should be facing north or northeast if possible. In a mirror of superstition in the western world, a spirit house should never be to the left of a doorway and should never be facing a road or a toilet.

Spirit houses are intended to provide a shelter for spirits that could cause problems for the people if not appeased. The shrines often include images or carved statues of people and animals. Votive offerings are left at the house to propitiate the spirits.

Thai culture is steeped in astrology and other forms of divination, such as palm reading, tarot cards, and feng shui, which all sit comfortably in the country's brand of Buddhism.

A lot of Thai people speak English, so that is helpful. Learning to speak Thai may take more than several years to get halfway there. So, since Saisampan speaks perfect English, there was no need for me to suffer for years to learn Thai. I only need Thai when I want to hitch a ride with a taxi. Even Thai-speaking taxi riders have trouble explaining in Thai where the driver is to take you. This happens because the taxi drivers come from upcountry and don't have the knowledge of how to navigate BKK's streets. The solution is to hire a knowledgeable Thai taxi driver and thus have a driver for your car when you need to go to a destination. Our driver works for us only on days when we need him, and we give him plenty of early warning. This deal serves him well and as well as us.

The social circle of Thai friends that Saisampan knows and continues to be introduced to mostly speak fluent English. So, my experience with these friends of Saisampan has been very positive, and whenever we gather for lunch or dinner, we have a lot of things to talk about. There is a different level of socializing, and that is attending a Thai funeral at one of the Temples, which has a proper gathering space for the mourners as well as a crematorium. A proper Thai funeral takes at least seven days, and normally, the gathering is early evening. It involves a lot of chanting, usually by six monks, and afterward, a lot of eating is quite normal, more or less like a wake. When the day arrives for the cremation, the family will make their farewell speeches and often provide a gratis memorial book with lots of photos of the deceased.

Whenever we meet socially, it always not only includes a meal, but it also includes exchanges of gifts, often of food items. Food plays a big role in Thai society and the question "have you eaten?" comes up regularly.

Food is indeed our main daily need, but to make the best of the day, you need to know that nothing is more health-oriented than a steady minimum of seven hours of sleep a night.

I say that because about four years ago, I read an interview in the weekend *Financial Times* about Matthew Walker, who studied sleep for thirty years at Berkeley. When I read his book, *Why We Sleep*, I learned a lot, but in the appendix of the book, there is a "list of twelve tips to healthy sleep." When I followed Walker's tips, I got rid of two very unpleasant sleep disturbances, which had interfered with my sleep for decades! Within six weeks of following the twelve tips, these effects were totally gone, and from then onward, I slept as soundly as a baby.

Here are the sleep disturbances that bothered me for years: 1) Restless leg syndrome, and 2) Recurring frustrating dreams about the same subject, e.g., losing my wallet, my car keys, my American Express checks, my suitcase, etc. I never lost anything at all but for those lousy dreams!

Why are we as American as apple pie? When I landed in America in August 1947, a slice of apple pie at a Horn and Hardart automat cost a quarter. At that time, shortly after WWII, there was no divisiveness in America. Instead, apple pie was the quintessential American product. It may be an apt metaphor. It was brought to America from foreign shores, was influenced by other cultures and immigration patterns, and spread through the world by global affairs. Perhaps if we focus our future on apple pie again, then we might again become as

American as apple pie, which takes us back under, for example, the Truman presidency. When Truman beat Dewey in 1947, it was a big upset, yet Americans were nevertheless as American as apple pie, and Governor Dewey in Albany, New York, acted accordingly by conceding to Truman. Let it be again that way. Amen.

I thank all the people who bought and read my autobiography. I hope you were amused as well as joyful passengers along all the travel I undertook for both my business and my pleasure! Following my trail would take another long life!

ARTWORK

Westerbork drawing

Westerbork drawing

Printed in Great Britain
by Amazon

14428263R00089